BYGON
RYE HARE

GW00492756

RYE MEMOR

Thomas Peacocke School Local History Group
Co-Ordinator and Editor: Jo Kirkham

INTRODUCTION

We have enjoyed putting together Information about Rye Harbour, but we could not have done it without many people's help.   In particular we must thank Mr Michael Alford, who has allowed us to reproduce his "History of Rye Harbour" and who has helped in many other ways.   The memories of Mrs Pope and Mrs Morphy give,   with the recollections of Miss Saunders, Mrs Gawn, Mrs Baldry, Mrs Caister and the others, a picture of a close knit, friendly village, whose independent, ingenious inhabitants have not always had an easy life, but who have welcomed visitors into their community. Indeed, I can vouch for that fact, as Rye Harbour people, (or 'Harbour Ducks' as some call themselves), made me and my family very welcome when we lived amongst them.

Jo Kirkham, Editor, 1992.

James Bennett, age 14, produced the cover drawings.

ISBN 1 870600 25 8: 2nd Revised Edition
2006

(ISBN 1 870600 15 0: 1st Edition)

Volume 18 in the Rye Memories Series

Printed in Great Britain by Adams of Rye Limited

INTRODUCTION TO NEW EDITION

This volume in the 'Rye Memories' series produced by the students of Thomas Peacocke Community College has been out of print for several years.

The steady flow of requests for a 'reprint' happily coincided with the establishment of Rye Harbour Heritage and it is an opportune time to prepare an updated volume, together with more illustrations, kindly provided by Dr Barry Yates from the Nature Reserve's archive, and fine line drawings by Brian Hargreaves which first appeared in 'Ryennium' – Rye at the Millennium', written by Jo Kirkham and published by Rye Town Council in 2000. Michael Alford has yet again supported the project and has updated his 'History of Rye Harbour'.

I extend my thanks to them and also to the members of Rye Harbour Heritage for their help and encouragement. Rye Harbour Heritage was established in 2005, around 200 years after the harbour's first settlement. It aims to record and promote the rich and varied history of Rye Harbour village, lying between the industrial area, the Harbour of Rye and the Nature Reserve, one of the best in East Sussex.

Rye Harbour Heritage

Rye Harbour
Nature Reserve

The reprint of this book was funded by Rye Harbour Nature Reserve and English Nature through Defra's Aggregates Levy Sustainability Fund. The proceeds will be divided between Thomas Peacocke Community College, to be used to buy books for the Library, and Rye Harbour Heritage.

Jo Kirkham: January 2006.

ENGLISH
NATURE

The Countryside Agency
Landscape
Access
Recreation

DEFRA'S AGGREGATES LEVY SUSTAINABILITY FUND GRANT SCHEME

CONTENTS

CHAPTER 1

A
SHORT HISTORY
OF
RYE HARBOUR
by Michael Alford

FOREWORD

When I first compiled and wrote these notes in 1966, I was working the suction dredge that was creating what is now 'Castle Water'.

I was operating the dredger, which comprised a seven-inch centrifugal gravel pump, powered by an eight cylinder 150 horse powered diesel engine by Davey-Paxmen of Colchester. Gwynes of Lincoln made the pumps.

Between the filling of the barges, each of which when loaded carried around 90 tons, there was usually a break of sometimes half an hour or so when, after essential maintenance and brass polishing of pipes and gauges, it provided the time in which these notes were written.

I had long been interested in the history of Rye Harbour and in my school days I had listened to the memories of older people. Much of this was stored inside my head, and was first published in 'Bygone Rye Harbour' in 1992.

I am grateful to Jo Kirkham for providing the opportunity for putting these notes into print, as no one else had been particularly interested before; Rye Harbour was considered a poor relation!

However, times have now changed and I wish the Heritage Group well in their endeavours. Finally, gravel extraction ceased in October 1969, and it took a long time for all of us to adjust to the outside world.   January 2006.

PART 1
1800 (approx) - 1840

The site on which the village of Rye Harbour stands was, towards the end of the 1790's and early 1800's, a very bleak and desolate spot.

The foreshore at that time was on the ridge of shingle on which the Martello Tower stands; beyond that, looking Southwards, was nothing but open sea. Clark, in his History of Rye published in 1861, tells us that "Just before the close of the last, (18th) century, there was not a house at this spot. The only inhabitant was a man whose name was John and, that being the case, he was called John-All-Alone. He lived alone, went to sea alone, was drowned alone, picked up alone and buried alone".

Whilst there were probably no houses here, no doubt there were a few huts in which long-shore fishermen kept their gear, and a map dated 1799 by Mudge, shows one or two buildings situated at 'The Point', which would have been used by the Excise and Revenue and the Rye Harbour Authorities at that time.

A little further inland on the mud flats opposite Messrs. Hall & Co's gravel and sand plant, remains can be seen of a house that was still in existence during the late 1870's. This was Stag House, and the area of land in the vicinity covered at very high tides was, and is, Stag's Hole. 'The Stag' was a revenue cutter that patrolled Rye Harbour mouth and Rye Bay in search of smugglers during the late 18th and early 19th century. Stag House was built for the crew and their families in order that the Excise and the Revenue might find it easier to keep an eye on shipping entering and leaving the port of Rye.

The burial records at St. Mary's Church, Rye, contain an entry recording the burials, on October 4th 1793, of John Hollows and Richard Oke, both aged 18, who were drowned whilst attempting to make harbour in a small boat belonging to 'The Stag', Captain Haddock, Master.

Around the year 1805, the possibility of invasion by Napoleon Bonaparte's forces was very real, and so, around the South East and East coast of England, a series of defences, known as Martello Towers were erected at an average cost of £20,000 each, which was quite a lot of money in those days.

Most of these Towers have disappeared, but the one at Rye Harbour still stands; a silent watcher over the years.

'The Enchantress' at Rye Harbour

Its official name is 'Enchantress', and its number is 28. After the Napoleonic Wars and during the time of the Coastal Blockade, it was used as a lock up for convicted smugglers being, during that time, under the supervision of the Admiralty and not the Army. The Blockade, an endeavour to check smuggling by intercepting smugglers at sea, was established in 1817. At this time smuggling at Rye was at such a height that a guard ship, 'H.M.S Enchantress', was placed in a dock on the West bank of the River Rother, opposite where the Church now stands, under the command of Lt. Bickens, RN. Long boats were used to intercept any ship or fishing boat that that Bickens suspected. Consequently a large number of arrests were made and Lt. Bickens became very unpopular: so much so that that he was waylaid and attacked in The Mint in Rye one evening, and was badly injured. Unfortunately for the attackers, they were recognised, arrested and sent to prison for five years.

The 'Enchantress' housed the wives and families of the seamen on board her, there being two entries in the Icklesham burial registers mentioning the ship's name and the names of the persons buried.

After the Coast Blockade was ended in 1834, the 'Enchantress' became the home of Coastguards and their families until the old Coastguard Cottages were built in 1861. The ship lingered on for a few more years and was sold to William Watson who broke her up.

Between 1833 and 1838 the last piece of innings occurred on Romney Marsh, and that by the Rye Harbour Commissioners on lands owned by them, over which high tides flowed.

The Rye Harbour Embankment Act, 1833, is of special interest to us, as it was mainly through it that Rye Harbour, as a village, really comes into being, thus being officially 'christened' with a name and provided with an access road along the run of the present one. Along where the Rye Harbour Road from Brede Sluice Bridge now runs, it was, prior to the innings by the erection of the present mud wall along the river bank, under water at high tides, just as it is today over Stags Hole and the mud flats South of the village.

The ditch running at the rear of Rye View was known, and still is occasionally, as Oyster Creek, it being, prior to embanking, a creek of considerable size running past the allotments towards Winchelsea Watch House.

The Coronation Field would also have been covered at high tides but, once the embankment was completed from the old level crossing to the North of the village in more or less a straight line to the Vicarage, an acreage of land became available for cultivation. The road now runs on top of this wall. Although it may seem hard to believe, it is a fact that small boats used Oyster Creek to lay up in during the winter months, especially in the vicinity where the road now passes. There was a ford across the creek, between where Rye View and the Inkerman Arms now stand. Oysters were also gathered there until the late 1870's, they being considered a delicacy by the gypsies, who used to pay periodic visits to collect both oysters and mussels, the mussels being collected from the river.

And how did people get to Rye Harbour before the road was built? Well, so far, this is not clear but, if tradition is correct, as more often than not it is, then the usual way for pedestrians would be over the ferry at Rock Channel, along the footpath towards Camber, and finally across the river by boat, or wade at low water. Alternately they could cross the River Brede and make their way roughly where the railway formerly ran, as the railway track has always been, by tradition, an unofficial right of way, and may thus have been the usual way.

For carts and horses, however, it was a different matter. Coming from Rye they would have to go towards Winchelsea Beach, and then along the track from Winchelsea Beach, past the Winchelsea Watch Houses, and eventually come out at Rye View, where they could either turn right and brave the ford or carry on straight across to where the 'Enchantress' lay. I should think, however, that the usual means of transport would have been by boat.

Finally in this first chapter, the first entry in the Icklesham registers mentioning Rye Harbour as such, was recorded on October 17th 1839, when William Gould, a customs officer, married Phoebe Welsted, whose father, James Welsted, was Foreman of Works at Rye Harbour. I should mention that, until 1903, when it became a separate parish, Rye Harbour came within the Parish of Icklesham for ecclesiastical purposes, and still is within Icklesham parish for civil affairs.

PART 2

During the first Chapter we have read how the village had grown from a collection of fishermen's huts and an Excise and Revenue Station in the early 1800's, until 1838, by which time a road had been built from Rye and the name 'Rye Harbour' had been given to the hitherto nameless settlement situated at the mouth of the River Rother.

Now we move into, comparatively speaking, more recent times - the 1840's and 1850's.

The mechanical age that was changing the face and way of life in Great Britain had, in a small way, already affected Rye Harbour and Rye for, during the years 1838 and 1839, two steam packet boats, the 'Windsor Castle' and the 'Edinburgh Castle' began to run between Rye and Boulogne to a regular schedule. Later on, in 1853, the first steam tug, 'The Erin', commenced work on the Rother.

The Port of Rye was an extremely busy place during the 1840's, with ships coming and going almost daily. An inn, 'The Ship', was opened at the Point and several houses were built in that area. The first general shop was opened at a house by the side of the 'Ship', and generally there appears to have been work at Rye Harbour for everyone - if they wanted it - either on the cargo boats, fishing at sea, or along the foreshore with keddle nets, lay-lines or shrimp nets, gathering cockles and oysters and, if any of these failed, the usual things to fall back on during the appropriate seasons were mushrooming, blackberrying and hop picking. Driftwood could be gathered, as it is today, along the foreshore to supplement the coal supplies. Whilst the inhabitants at Rye Harbour during this time were not by any means rich, they were able to live and survive at a time when thousands were starving throughout England.

In 1845 plans were made for Rye Harbour to be made into a Cross Channel port by the South East Railway Company, and several different plans were, about this time, under consideration by the Railway Company. One was for the line to run along the East bank of the Rother, joining with the Hastings - Ashford line near Craven Bridge. This was a period known as the Railway Mania Era, when hundreds of fantastic plans for railways were proposed and fortunes were made and lost. The final plans decided upon were passed by Parliament in 1845, and these provided, not for a Cross Channel port, as at first envisaged, but a Quay for coal and general merchandise and a single track line running from the West of the railway bridge over the Tillingham at Rye, on the Ashford and Hastings line.

The Quay known as the Admiralty Quay, and the line were constructed during 1853 and both were opened for use during March 1854. The Admiralty Quay had upon it a weigh bridge and a steam crane and they were, as well as the railway, in regular use for many years.

The East Pier stone works were, during 1854, extended and straightened towards the Harbour entrance, making it easier for shipping entering and leaving the Harbour. Much of this work is being renewed at the present time by the Kent River Authority, some of the original having survived since the 1830's.

With the growth of the village during the 1840's, the need became apparent to provide for the spiritual well being of both inhabitants and visiting seamen. The Reverend H. W. Churton, who had been appointed Vicar of Icklesham in 1843, made efforts towards getting support in building a small Church, the need being very great. His efforts were rewarded for, on March 29th 1849, the foundation stone was laid by William Drew Lucas Shadwell amidst great rejoicing. Mr Shadwell owned an estate between Fairlight and the Rother, and Rye Harbour was included in it. Mr Lucas Shadwell in his time did much good amongst the people on his estate, as did Mrs Lucas Shadwell, who carried on the good works, both being examples of Christian living to us all.

During the Summer of 1849 work proceeded steadily on the new Church and finally, on August 29th 1849, came the great day when the Church was consecrated by the Bishop of Chichester. This is how that happy day was described in the Sussex Express, August 31st, 1849 :-

'Rye Harbour New Church

on Thursday last, situated at Rye Harbour Point, about 3½ miles from Winchelsea and 2 from Rye, was consecrated by the Bishop of Chichester and opened for divine service. Many of the clergy and laity of the neighbourhood attended and the day was remarkably fine, it being a pleasing sight to notice the different groups in vehicles and on foot, hastening across the soft green sward and heavy shingle towards the Church which, being small, was expected to be much crowded. On arrival at the spot the 'Pelican', a man of war gun brig, was observed to have her rigging gaily decorated with flags of various sizes, shapes and colours. In the Churchyard also were red, blue, green and white flags of a humbler description bearing on them the words 'prayer', 'praise', grace', 'faith' etc. The houses of the coastguards and others were similarly decorated with flags of various descriptions.

At 11, the Bishop and his Chaplain approached the Church and were met accordingly in the usual form by the Chancellor, Dr Phillimore, the Vicar and some of the Clergy. After consecration of Church and Yard, morning service for the occasion was read by the Reverend H. W. Churton, and the Bishop preached a plain but impressive sermon. His lordship showed that though no visible outward token of the Divine Presence was now to be expected, yet that promise 'two or three gathered together' etc., assured us of

His Presence now with fully as much certainty to those who trust His word. After the service, the greater part of those who had come from a distance proceeded on board the 'Pelican', the deck of which had been tastefully prepared by Lt. Stanbury, R.N., who kindly lent his ship for the reception of up to 100 guests who sat down to an elegant luncheon. At 3.15 the tables were cleared and reset for a dinner for coastguards and others to the numbers of 60-70. At 4.15 a large number had re-assembled for the afternoon service. Prayers were read by the Reverend W. Clarke of Winchelsea and an able and interesting sermon was preached by Archdeacon Hare upon Psalm xxxiv verse 10, showing that we should regard the House of God as our spiritual home, our best, our most lasting home on earth.

The Church now opened was commenced on March 29th, 1849. The style is neat early gothic. Mr Tevlon of London is the Architect, Mr J. Judge of Rye the builder. Mr Thomas, organist of Rye, attended with his choir from that place and presided at the harmonium, a small accordion organ, built by Mr Luff of Brighton and kindly furnished by Mr Henry, brother of Mr W. D. Lucas Shadwell, donor of the site of the church.'

The Church, dedicated to the Holy Spirit, is built of blue local stone with Caen stone groins and mouldings. The estimated cost being £933.11 shillings 8 pence. Samuel Tevlon, the architect, was in charge of the restoration work at St. Nicholas, Icklesham a year or so previously. He also designed Holy Trinity Church, Robertson Street, Hastings, Netherfield Church, near Battle, Icklesham (Old) School, and the old school at Rye Harbour appears also to be his design.

I think that this just about covers the important events up to 1850. In the next chapter we will look at events from 1850 to 1900.

PART 3

Following the consecration and opening of the Church of the Holy Spirit at Rye Harbour, the Church seems to have settled down to a fairly quiet existence for the next 50 years or so. The Sunday service was usually at 3 p.m. conducted by either Mr. Churton or his curate, who came from Icklesham, usually in a pony and cart and occasionally walking across the fields.

The first burial took place on November 28th 1852, being the body of Sarah Elizabeth Cowell, aged 5, who was drowned in a shipwreck. The weather at that period had been very stormy with high winds causing trouble to shipping in the English Channel.

In 1852 two lifeboat stations were opened, one on each side of Rye Harbour mouth, in order that shipping in the vicinity in distress might be best served, either by one or the other station, according to circumstances. For identification purposes, the station on the West main was known as the Winchelsea Station and the one on the East main at Camber was known as the Rye Lifeboat Station. Although two different stations and crews, they both came under the one committee and, until their closures, did excellent work in saving the lives of mariners.

So far I have not been able to discover the names of the first lifeboats, or their crews, but the late Jim Downey, at one time the coxswain of the Winchelsea boat, told me that when he was young he was told that the Winchelsea boat was manned mainly by coastguards from Winchelsea Watch houses.

During the year 1859, Messrs. Lee and Sons, who were engaged on building works at Dover Harbour, erected, at the West end of Tram Road, a works to manufacture concrete blocks weighing 4-6-8 tons for shipping to Dover, either by lighter or by rail, for the construction of sections of the harbour. This works appears to have been of considerable size, judging from the remains left, and lasted for almost 20 years, after which the boiler house, the pump house, the stables and part of the workshops were converted to private houses and are still used as such today. Remains of the concrete beds upon which the blocks were made, now provide very solid foundations for several houses at the North West of Tram Road.

Incidentally, the name Tram Road originated from the tram road constructed from the works to the railway and to the Admiralty Quay. The embankment along which the rails were laid remains to this day and can be seen between the council houses and along the path by the side of Martin's shop, to the Point. A further spur ran past the front of houses at the Point to a jetty near to the present slipway.

Another event in 1859 took place on May the 13th of that year, when the first stone was laid for a school, over which the coastguards fired several volleys in honour of the donors to such a worthy and noble cause. The ground on which the school stood and the field were donated by W. D. Lucas Shadwell Esq. It is ironical to record that 94 years later, in 1953, the village was to purchase by public subscription, the former playing field of the school, it having fallen into private hands.

About this time also the 'Inkerman Arms' was opened and Inkerman Terrace was built. The owner of the 'Inkerman Arms' was Edward White, a pilot of the Port of Rye. His grave and stone are in the Church Yard. The 'William the Conqueror Inn' must also have opened about this time. So far as I can trace, William Watson and a man named Waters were the owners, whilst the 'Ship Inn' was owned by a family named Ditton.

With the commencement of the concrete works, the opening, in 1860, of a brickyard where the timber wharf is to be, [now J. Alsford Ltd. Ed.] the various shipping activities and two lime kilns by the side of the river meant that Rye Harbour at that time was a very busy spot. Houses were erected for employees of Lee & Sons and a new shop and Post Office were open within a year or two, the owners being Henbrey, afterwards Bucknell. The shop is now two private houses - River View 1 and 2.

Another event of 1860 was the opening of the Institute Reading Rooms and Sailors' Home. Mr Lucas Shadwell erected the building entirely at his own expense. Tradition says that the Institute was opened as a counter attraction for the three drink shops that, at that time, with the influx of workmen, must have been doing a very brisk trade, there being no other place for workmen and seamen to go in their spare time.

The Institute, for many years, also provided temporary accommodation for shipwrecked seamen, facilities being provided for that purpose and a caretaker living on the premises; the first being, so far as I can discover, a Mrs Rubis, a widow of a seaman of the port. Whilst the need for shipwrecked victims has declined in these days of power driven ships, in those days, the Institute served a most worthy cause as being a mariner was then a most hazardous occupation, fraught with danger, as the burial records of Icklesham, Winchelsea and Rye show. The words 'drowned at sea' occur on almost every page during the 19th Century.

Although the offering of refuge to the shipwrecked has ceased to play an important part in the village's life, the Institute still is useful in providing the accommodation for the Men's Club, or for the Sunday School and other meetings, religious or secular. Its sleeping accommodation is often in demand during the summer months for Church youth clubs, Scouts or Guides for their annual camp. This shows that the Institute, although 107 years old, is still as useful as when it first opened.

When the concrete works commenced production, a spur was made on the railway running to the shingle beds where Messrs. Hall and Co. now work. This provided the aggregates for making the concrete. The men on this work were paid on a piece work basis; two men loading two trucks a day, using shovels and wheelbarrows gained an average weekly earning of 16 shillings. It then appears that the trucks were shunted to the Point and the ballast was off loaded onto the Tram Road trolleys and towed to the works. Alternately, ballast may have been loaded into river barges at Nook Beach, floated up the river to the jetty in front of the Conqueror and then off loaded onto the trolleys.

Before leaving the 19th Century, you may be interested in two murders. The first was of a child whose body was uncovered by a dog and discovered by people returning from Church on April 1st, 1854. The Inquest was held in the 'Ship Inn' and the surgeon said that the medical evidence showed that the child had been born with a person or persons assisting, after which it had been strangled and buried at a spot where the Institute now stands. A verdict of murder by persons unknown was recorded.

The second occurred on the line opposite to where Weslake's now stands, where John White, a labourer at the concrete works, strangled his wife and put her in a ditch there where she remained for three days. She was discovered by a boy walking to Rye to collect the mails. White was tried at the Assizes, where the Jury, taking a just and merciful view of the circumstances, gave a verdict of manslaughter. He was sentenced to be transported for life. From accounts of the trial, White had a bad tempered and nagging wife and on this occasion was provoked beyond endurance, as she had been continuously 'at him' for several days.

15

During the next few years, the various industries carried on their different works, some years being good and some bad. The Church and Institute had a fairly uneventful existence, performing useful services all the same. Mr Budden and his wife taught the young at the school. The brickyard closed down in 1874 and the concrete works about 1880.

The Chemical Works opened in 1879, a company called the 'Rye Chemical and Manufacturing Company', being the proprietors. Tar was the material used for processing at the works and many boat loads of pitch left the jetty erected by the side of the works, over the years. One notable event concerning the Chemical Works was a fire that occurred on one Sunday evening; some oil in the boiler house being the cause. The fire swept right through the works, there being little that the Volunteer Fire Brigade could do, apart from digging a trench around the place to prevent the pitch and tar from spreading and causing further damage.

A rather peevish note is recorded in the Icklesham burial records during 1882. It records the burial of a child, Rosetta Murphy, aged 15 months, with a note saying that 'The burial service was conducted by a Roman priest from some Church over at St. Leonards'. Rye and Rye Harbour and much of the surrounding district was, at that time, in the Roman Catholic parish of St. Leonards on Sea, but that, however, is another story.

I was told many years ago by an old lady that, for a time, there was a small group of Catholic coastguards who, in the course of duty, came together with their families at Rye Harbour and subsequently held prayer meetings together in each others houses.

The allotment gardens were in use during the 1870's and the coastguards had gardens opposite the Inkerman Terrace. Whilst the coastguard's gardens have now been built on, the allotments are still giving good service to those who work them, most of the vacant plots being cultivated by Mr Frank Saunders, a farmer.

Towards the end of the 19th Century, several houses were erected along the main road; William Watson erecting Pains Cottages and The Square during the 1880's and Marshall Ames of Rye building several others almost opposite. Martello House was built in Tram Road from bricks taken from No. 31 Martello Tower at Winchelsea

Beach. This Tower, being undermined by the sea, was dismantled for the thousands of bricks it contained. Also during the 1890's, the school was extended and a works making paving slabs was fully operating, its owners being Elliots of Hastings. Some of their slabs can be seen in Rye, especially around Church Square and Watchbell Street. The name 'Elliot' is let into the slab in brass letters.

This then is the end of the chapter dealing with the main happenings in the second half of the 19th Century. I think that I have covered most of the items of interest although practically every item contains a history in itself that is well worth investigating at some future date.

PART 4

The 20th Century opens with life much the same as in the late 19th Century.

The Admiralty Quay was unused, but the West Quay was in regular use, Caen stone being in demand for road making. This was the principal commodity discharged at that time. Blue flints were gathered along the shore. Those engaged in that occupation, having a small boat carrying between 2 and 5 tons, would sail their vessel to a point along the fore shore or near the river's mouth, where they intended gathering the flints and beach together.

The flints were picked off the beach by hand into trays and, when full, would be carried by the boulderer, as the collector was usually known and, by means of yokes, were emptied into his boat. At the end of the day, or when his boat was loaded, which ever the case was, he would, when the tide was correct, sail back into harbour and run ashore.

He proceeded to unload the flints or boulders onto his pile, this procedure being repeated by the boulderman until, collectively, there was enough for a shipload to be carried to either Runcorn or Selby.

At those ports they were loaded onto railway trucks or the narrow boats for shipment to the Potteries where they were used in various processess and still are, from other sources, in pottery work. The 'Gleunen' of Runcorn was often engaged on the work, bringing a shipment of coal into Rye and loading the flints at the West Quay and returning to Runcorn. Messrs. Vidler and Sons vessels usually delivered via Selby.

The payment received by the boulder men at this time was 3/6 per ton; a ton being 22 cwt to allow for impurities among the flints.

The living was near starvation at times but, as there was not much else there being a surplus of labour over employment, it was better than nothing. Incidentally, those who did shrimping received 2d a pint at that time.

In about 1900, after a fairly quiet existence for 50 years, the spiritual life at Rye Harbour came into prominence. Plans were in hand to divorce Rye Harbour from Icklesham and make it a separate parish together with Camber. Mrs. Lucas Shadwell at that time, and until her death, did a tremendous amount of good in the village for the spiritual and material well being of the inhabitants and, with Rye Harbour to have its own Vicar, Mrs Shadwell generously built a Vicarage entirely at her own expense.

On the present site of the Vicarage there was, prior to building, a large hole, possibly excavated by Lee & Sons, to make up the embankment for their 'Tram Road' from the works to the river.

During the hard winter of 1901, with fishing and boating activities at a standstill, Mrs Shadwell gave employment to the men of the village at 2/6 a day to fill the hole with mud from the puggling (mudflats), after which the Vicarage was built in preparation for the new Vicar.

I should mention that Mrs Lucas Shadwell was a very active worker in the cause of Temperance and wrote many books with this movement in mind. Mrs Shadwell had, a year or two previously to 1901, bought out the 'Ship Inn', closed it down and turned it into a private dwelling house just as today, with Dick Hunt being the last proprietor of the establishment.

To return to the Church affairs however, the new Vicar, the Reverend Montague Manning, took up his duties in 1903. Mr Manning appears to have been of the evangelical type of clergyman, for we have record of revival meetings at the Institute with evangelical men of the period, Messrs Torry Alexander and others. The 'Band of Hope' was in full swing and on several occasions 'The Gospel Ship' was berthed at Rye Harbour, upon which gospel revival meetings were held.

In all these various works Mrs Shadwell took a leading part and, it is hoped, much good was affected. Another character very much to the fore at these times was Mr Maltby who, with his steam tug the 'Princess May of London' and a team of Whitstable divers, were salvaging what they could from the 'La Panto', a steam vessel that sunk after a collision in Rye Bay. Mr Maltby was, together with Mr Watson, one of the village grocers, engaged in political rallying around the district. The three are still remembered by the older people leaving Rye Harbour for meetings in Mr Watson's pony and trap, wearing rosettes as 'big as dinner plates'.

A Methodist Church was erected in 1901 and was served from Rye during its period of use.

The only other incident to recall during the Reverend Montague Manning's incumbency was a Consistory Court held in the Church during 1903, on account of Mr Manning making certain Church alterations without obtaining the Faculty from the Bishop authorising him to do so. This matter was settled to the general satisfaction of all parties and Mr Manning stayed as Vicar until 1908, when his place was taken by the Reverend F. G. Rochfort Wade, who stayed until 1915.

It was in Mr Rochfort Wade's incumbency that efforts were made to have the Churchyard enlarged, as it had had to be closed for burials, being full. The first mention of the need for an enlarged Churchyard had occurred at the 1908 Vestry Meeting, but some years were to pass before the enlargement was effected, due to inaction of various authorities concerned, for we again hear of the matter in 1913 when we read of 'the grave concern of the rate payers over the continued delay of providing a suitable area'. The Church was enlarged during 1912.

Another notable feature established by Mr Rochfort Wade and his family, was a charity which, every so often, pays a small sum of money to the four oldest men and the four oldest women who were born and are still living in the village.

To turn to secular events in Rye Harbour, main drainage and water was provided about the year 1912 by the Rural District Council. Several more houses were erected in the village and the digging and carrying of shingle to Dover by rail ceased. The workings of the last

Contractors towards the old Lifeboat House can still be seen today, providing a useful stretch of water for web footed birds.

The Great War of 1914-18 saw a number of men leave for active service, some never to return. During the period of hostilities many of those left behind were engaged in coastal defences and watching services along the shoreline. One or two bombs were dropped near to the Chemical Works, at that time owned by Messrs. Forbes Abbot and Leonard - a name many older persons will recall - they being, in their time, model employers.

To return to bombs, one bomb crater served a useful purpose to one Rye Harbour man as at that same time a donkey of his had died and so it was pushed into the hole and buried, saving him the job of digging a hole - not being quite the thing that Kaiser Bill had in mind for his bombs.

The West Quay fell into disuse at some period during the war and was consequently partly dismantled, the steam crane upon it being sold to the Chemical Works. Consequent to the West Quay being closed, blue flints, whose price incidentally had risen due to hostilities to £1 per ton, were dispatched by rail, this being the usual method until the trade ceased.

To go back to 1915. A new Vicar, the Reverend G. Haydn Evans, was appointed in that year to succeed the Reverend Rochfort Wade. The Methodist Church meanwhile had declined in its membership and Mr Haydn Evans managed to raise the money by public subscription to purchase it for use by the Scouts, Guides and for other suitable activities, as befitting a building that had once been dedicated for worship. The Mission Room, as it is known, is regularly used for various village activities to this date. The Reverend Haydn Evans did not have a great deal of use out of the Mission Room however, for, in October 1918, he moved on to other work and was succeeded by the Reverend W. March, who was inducted on November 20th 1918.

PART 5

After the 1914-18 War many who had served in the forces returned to civilian life, but a great many did not return at all, having given their lives in battle.

The first major item of interest is the erection of a War Memorial to those who had served and an additional marble tablet, inside the Church on the South wall, to those who had fallen. The War Memorial is a lych gate at the entrance to the Churchyard, with the names of all those who had served in the armed forces, including those who had been killed. These were completed and dedicated in 1920 before a gathering of parishioners and local personalities, including the Mayor of Rye, Alderman Jesse Deacon, and Lady Maud Warrender of Leasam House.

About this time also, Mrs Lucas Shadwell died and went to her eternal reward. The Reverend W. March stayed until 1923, when he was succeeded by the Reverend E. S. Warner, who was inducted on May 12th of that year.

Turning for a moment to every day affairs, there were several changes in employment after the Great War. The West Quay was no longer in use by commercial shipping. The whole Port of Rye was less used than previously, due to the tendency towards larger ships in the commercial shipping world. Fishing, though still important, was not so prominent as it had been in previous years. The blue boulder industry, though still continuing, was less profitable than during the Great War and, for the first time, people went out of the village to their daily employment in larger numbers than hitherto. A bus service was started in 1923 by Messrs. Wright and Pankhurst of Rye and ran to and from Rye several times daily. At first buses were used, but the Rye Harbour Road was getting in a bad state of repair and the buses had so many springs broken through this, that motor lorries with a canvas tilt covering the passengers were used. Wooden seats were placed round the sides of the lorry for the passengers to sit on.

When repairs were done on the road, buses were used again. Messrs. Wright and Pankhurst ran the service until selling part of their service, in 1931, to the East Kent Road Car Co. Ltd., who are operators of the bus service to this day. The Rye - Rye Harbour service being their service 115. [1966. Ed.]

It is interesting to note in the Church registers the change in occupation during the 1920's from previous years. Whereas the main occupations of persons recorded around 1900 were coastguards, mariners or fishermen, those of the 1920's have less connection with the sea, such as motor driver, brick layer or farmworker.

There is little to record during the Reverend E. S. Warner's stay as Vicar of Rye Harbour. The only item of interest being the Royal Humane Society's Certificate being presented to Richard (Dick) Cutting by Mrs Warner for having saved the life of the Vicar from drowning during September 1924.

Dick Cutting, as some of his family before him, ran a ferry from Rye Harbour across the river to Camber and people often used the ferry in conjunction with the Rye and Camber Tram. Both the ferryman and the Tram Company could issue tickets for either service. Dick ran the ferry until 1944 when war work brought it to a close.

The Reverend H. Newton succeeded the Reverend E. Warner in 1927, being inducted on October 15th. Just over a year later, on the morning of November 14th 1928, the Rye Harbour Lifeboat, as it was now officially called, put to sea in a whole S.W. gale . . . .

A Memorial to the crew was dedicated in the Churchyard on November 17th 1931, a tablet of Manx stone inside the Church having been previously unveiled by Sir Claude Hill, Governor of the Isle of Man, on 24th June 1929. The loss of the lifeboat crew was also a severe blow to the already declining fishing and boating trades, from which it was to take years to recover. After the disaster, the Lifeboat Station was temporarily closed and later permanently closed.

The 'Mary Stanford' was taken to London by lorry, where she was broken up. Shortly after the closure of the Lifeboat Station, the Coastguard Station also closed down. The Watch House and the Officer's House and the Coastguard's Cottages were used by the workmen employed at Simpson's sand and gravel plant, situated next to the Church. The works had opened during the Spring of 1921.

About this time also the Harbour was given a thorough dredging by a Dutch dredging company, this work making a great and lasting improvement for shipping.

Also during the early 1930's, a wall was erected running parallel to the East Pier, thereby making a straight run of navigation between Rye Harbour Village and the sea.

The East Pier was extended about 1936 and it was during this work that a lighter loaded with concrete blocks, made by Lee & Sons, was discovered under the sand.

A works manufacturing concrete products was opened in 1936 and a little later on, a manufactory of brick and tiles. This was to close two or three years later and to be absorbed by Spun Concrete Ltd.

Another gravel pit was opened during 1936 by Messrs. John Carter of Baldslow. The plant for processing the materials was erected a little later and was situated next to the Chemical Works, which in that year was taken over from Forbes Abbot and Leonard by the South Eastern Tar Distillers Ltd. of Tonbridge.

A fair amount of gravel was being taken away from Rye Harbour by sea at that time, a jetty being erected for this purpose on the river bank opposite Messrs. Simpsons works. The Rye-Rye Harbour Road however was in a deplorable condition due to the increased heavy traffic from the various works, so much so, that buses ceased to run until the concrete road was built in 1937 or 38.

It is curious that whilst road making aggregates were being taken from Rye Harbour at that time, to various parts of East Sussex for the building of roads, that the only access road should have been neglected for so long.

At the Parish Church Council meeting held on 15th July 1936, it was stated that repairs to the Church roof were needed. Two builders had promised to come but had failed to do so. It was therefore resolved to contact Mr Miller of Rye. Electric lighting was installed during the same year at an approximate cost of £20.

The Reverend H. Newton's last Sunday as Vicar was on September 5th 1936, he being succeeded by the Reverend C. V. Dory who was inducted on February 25th 1937. On 15th March of that year the P.C.C. resolved that Mr F. Saunders make enquiries for soil for the new portion of the Churchyard. A year later in 1938 the Church was redecorated in chocolate and cream, at an approximate cost of £32. Also a vote of thanks was given to the Vicar of Belmont in Surrey and Miss Andrew, for gifts of hangings and fittings. The Church flagstaff was also attended to.

With the outbreak of war in 1939, a number of evacuées from London were billeted in the district and with them a Mr King Smith, who the registers note, was doing good work with the choir. The registers also record the disappointing attendance at morning service on Sundays. The numbers at evening service were maintained, but no increase was seen. Later, in 1940, with the situation on the Continent becoming more and more serious every day, the evacuées had left the district, to be followed, after the fall of France, by large numbers of local inhabitants of Rye Harbour and Rye.

Those who stayed behind were restricted to the immediate vicinity of the village, the shore being closed to almost everyone except shrimpers or Catchment Board workers.

The blue flint trade came to an end along the shore, Messrs. Hall & Co., who now owned Simpson's gravel pit, being the only people to send flints away to the Potteries. Mine fields were laid near to the coastline with the danger of invasion imminent. The 'William the Conqueror Inn' had closed for the duration of the war and bus services were cut to three a day. The school had closed at the end of June with the general evacuation, never to open again, Mrs Desmond being the last Headmistress. During the war years, the school was used as a cook house by the various regiments stationed at Rye Harbour.

On August 15th 1940 it was announced that the Reverend C. V. Dois was leaving Rye Harbour to take over a parish in Brighton, this parish being, due to evacuations, thinly populated. The Vicar of the Brighton Parish had joined H.M. Forces meantime, and arrangements had been made for the Rye Harbour Church to be served by the Rye clergy.

For a time however, in late 1940, services were conducted by an Army chaplain, the Reverend Max Gregory C.F., followed by a succession of chaplains. During 1941 and 1942 services were very spasmodic, but 1943 opens with Mr F. Saunders, a Churchwarden giving Bible readings at 3.15 on Sundays while, shortly afterwards, we read of the Church again being served from Icklesham by the Vicar, the Reverend W. Hilton Wright and occasionally from Rye. The service was usually held at 3.15, but often there was a poor attendance. Mr Hilton Wright managed as best he could, the congregation and helpers being only a small handful.

Meanwhile fishing had returned to the village in a big way, boats coming from all parts of the country and fortunes were made and lost by many engaged in the occupation. Several bombs were dropped in the village and a few houses were destroyed, two women being killed in one house. Many empty houses were used by N.C.O's and the Vicarage by the officers commanding the various companies stationed in the village.

With the end of the war, on May 6th 1945, the village was decorated with flags and bunting and, shortly afterwards, a service of thanksgiving was held at the Church. With the cease of hostilities and the gradual demobilisation of service personnel, the various houses used by the military came into use again as private dwellings. The Martello Tower, used during the War by the Royal Observer Corps, was vacated by them and fishing once again gradually declined.

A concrete road was built to the Point by the Catchment Board during 1946, several German prisoners of war working upon it. The road was extended to Winchelsea Beach during 1947, Mears Bros. being the contractors for this second road. Previous to the building of the two roads, a narrow gauge industrial railway ran along approximately the same route - being owned by the same authority as still owns the roads today. Messrs. Mears Bros. established a depot near to the level crossing during 1946. In later years they manufactured concrete buildings on the same site, trading under the name of Precon Ltd., until they closed down at the end of 1964.

A brick and tile works was established by Ightham Brick and Tile Company next to Messrs. John Carter's beach works during 1947. This ran until about 1952 when the buildings were sold to the Atlas Stone Co. who now manufacture concrete building blocks.

On March 28th, the Reverend Jason Battersby was inducted by the Bishop of Chichester and, once again, the spiritual life of the parish returned to normal. The various religious societies and works came to life again after the war.

During 1948 an officer of the Church Army, Captain Barlow and his wife, arrived to take charge of the Institute, youth work and various other parish activities. The Reverend J. Battersby was not enjoying the best of health. Both Captain and Mrs Barlow were an almost immediate success, both of them being the type of person who could get on with anyone.

During 1948 a Women's Institute Branch was founded and this excellent body is still flourishing today - holding its meetings in the Mission Room monthly.

A Men's Club was also formed at about the same time which is also flourishing today, snooker and billiards tournaments being played regularly during the Winter months in the same venue.

The road through the village was also made up during that year. The Reverend J. Battersby resigned from the living in 1951 due to ill health and was succeeded by the Reverend George Hill in September that year. November 4th was Captain and Mrs Barlow's last Sunday at Rye Harbour. Originally they came for twelve months but stayed for three years, everyone being sorry to see them go. Captain and Mrs Barlow were retiring from full time work and were settling in Hastings and so they were seen in the village several times during the years that followed.

During August 1953 special services were held to commemorate the 100th anniversary of the first rescue of the then Winchelsea Lifeboat. This service was attended by the Governor of the Isle of Man, who unveiled two boards placed on the North wall of the inside of the Church, giving a list of rescues made by the lifeboats until the disaster of 1928. The Bishop of Lewes officiated and representatives from the R.N.L.I. Headquarters attended, together with lifeboatmen from Hastings and Dungeness.

In 1953, being the year of Queen Elizabeth's Coronation, a suggestion was made that the old School Green be purchased to commemorate the event, beside providing a village playing field. A committee was formed, funds were raised and the field was duly named the Coronation Field, it being village property for all time.

In 1956 the Reverend G. Hill left Rye Harbour to work in Nottingham, where, a year or two afterwards, he was killed holding onto a bus whilst riding his bicycle.

Also in 1956 the Institute was completely re-roofed, tiles replacing the former slates, and the paint work was attended to.

The Reverend G. Hill's place at Rye Harbour was taken by the Reverend P. Smith who came from Norfolk. Mr Smith's stay was only to be of brief duration as, unfortunately, he died of pneumonia less than a year after being inducted. He was a man much liked by all who knew him.

The Reverend P. Smith's successor was the Reverend D. Patterson who arrived in 1957. It was during his stay, that the Church stone work was completely overhauled in 1959. The interior was completely redecorated, oak paneling being placed around the lower walls having a very pleasing effect on the eye. The interior work was carried out by Goddard Bros. of Rye. Mr E. Goddard was one of the Churchwardens and Mr G. Caister the other. Work on the stone was done by Messrs. Percy E. Link of Rye and Hastings. Part of Tram Road was surfaced during April 1957.

The fishing fleet had declined from the end of the war to one or two boats, but now has increased to 8 or 9 boats, working from the Fishmarket, Rye, where new jetties have been recently erected.

Yachting and pleasure boating is very popular at Rye Harbour, especially during the Summer. At the present time (1966), commercial shipping has decreased to one or two boat loads of timber a year delivered into Rye. Plans are going ahead to erect a timber wharf near to the old Admiralty Quay.

PART 6

AN UPDATE IN 1992

CHURCH

The Reverend E. Wilkinson was inducted by the Bishop of Lewes on St. George's Day 1966. A notable feature of the service was the presence of the clergy of the Free Churches in Rye and Father Richard of the Roman Catholic Church, it being, so far as is known, the first time that ministers of several denominations have gathered together at Rye Harbour during a service.

In April 1982, Rye Harbour became the 3rd member of new Team Ministry, with Rye and Playden and Canon John Williams took charge. Sadly he died suddenly and Canon David Maundrell took over. The Reverend Paddy Buxton is the present incumbent.

LAND USE

John Carter's was a gravel pit which closed on December 31 1970 and which has become Castle Water - a leisure site with workshop complex.

Altas Stone has become ARC. The Solvent Works, opened in 1960 by Smith Bros. on the site of a tar distillery, is still operating as part of C.M.R. Mears Bros. eventually went bankrupt and is now Long Products.

The zig zag in the Rye Harbour road caused by the old railway crossing was smoothed out about 1972.

J. Alsford's Timber Wharf opened in April 1968 and is still in action. Spun Concrete is a going concern. Hall & Co. closed down about 8 or 9 years ago and the site is vacant. Gould's Concrete Works were taken over by Henry Neal's company 'Caxton's Concrete'. This went bankrupt over the Canary Wharf scheme in October 1990.

HOUSING

The Mary Stanford Green housing estate of Council Houses was built between 1976-7. Many of the houses are now privately owned.

LIFEBOAT

An Inshore Lifeboat was placed at Rye Harbour in 1966, based in a shed near the slipway. A new shed for it was built about 1982. It is a very busy station, now concerned with tourists - especially rescuing those in trouble on inflatables and an offshore wind.

NATURE RESERVE

In 1974 the East Sussex County Council, together with Southern Water, (now N.R.A.), who own much of the land, established a Nature Reserve. It is becoming of national importance. It has a variety of interest but mainly sea birds and plants of shingle and salt marsh. There is a breeding colony of Little Terns and it is an important stop for migrating birds.

RYE HARBOUR AS A HARBOUR 1992

The future of the Harbour is under discussion at present. It is run by the National Rivers Authority, but privatisation is an option being seriously considered. The function of the Harbour as a flood control agent, especially in an area where so much land is below sea level, must be recognised as vital.

The latest figures for the use of Rye Harbour are from 1990/91.

These show that :-
1. 105 ships displacing 400 - 2000 tonnes visited. (Potential 500 ships.)
2. 43 fishing boats use the Harbour, with 26 crewed full time. It is the largest fishing fleet in the South East with a turnover of £2M per annum.
3. Approx. 800 yachts and motor vessels.
4. Approx. 1500 trailed sailing boats. The National Rivers Authority owns about a half of the berths and moorings available.

HARBOUR MASTERS
A Mr Coote was H.M. until his death in about 1935/6. His office was in a wooden building by the Landgate Steps in Rye itself. He was replaced by Mr Jack Doust who retired in about 1969. Mr Colin Marsh then took over and his deputy, Mr Carl Bagwell, became the present holder of the post.

FUTURE
There have been several scares about 'Development', including various schemes for marinas. The Yacht Club, the Golf Club and the land next to the Timber Wharf have permissions, but the financial climate is not favourable.

PART 7

AN UPDATE IN 2006

CHURCH
The Reverend Martin Sheppard became the incumbent from 1995 to 2003, and he arranged for the Church to become a Chapel of Ease to St. Mary's, Rye. The building has been modified so that, in addition to Services, it can become a venue for Arts and Drama. The Reverend Hugh Moseley is now the Rector.

LAND USE

Alsford's Wharf is now run by Rastrum. Hall & Co.'s is just an empty space, but the owners, Simpson & Gould, Rye Harbour Ltd. let out the water there for angling. ARC land is empty. Long Products have re-opened as Long and Cinque Ports Industry, producing insulation for pipes. Spun Concrete's land is gradually being cleared by Michael Hodgson to make Pine Furniture. Weslake's is now an electronics firm.

HOUSING

An area that succeeded in being a positive development is the area now called Lucas Shadwell Way and Oyster Creek. It used to be a factory that made concrete beams for flats and houses. Now it is the home to many new incomers and older inhabitants as well as giving the children of the Harbour somewhere to play.

The Institute (the old Methodist Chapel) has recently been sold and is now a private house.

LIFEBOAT

The Lifeboat House was extended and modernised in 1995.

RYE HARBOUR AS A HARBOUR 2006

The Environment Agency has taken over from the National Rivers Authority to run the Harbour.

From April 2005 to the present, (Jan 9 2006), 37 commercial ships have visited the Harbour and 53,610 tonnes of cargo dealt with.

I am watching with interest the **Sea Defence Bund** being built, keeping us safe from flooding and, as a side product, we are getting a new lake for birds to migrate to.

The local shop unfortunately deteriorated because of competition of larger stores and bad management and sadly it was shut down about 1995. The Rye Partnership, who bought the building and site, encouraged its re-opening. The community supported this and, with a little ceremony, it came alive again, with Bogden and Dot Wujek on the helm and it is doing very well.

We also now have a half-hourly **bus service** to Rye, via Tilling Green (No 325).

We look forward with hope that the village will flourish, but will retain its unique identity. There has been a big drive to involve the youth in the village growth so they feel part of its growth and heritage.

Children of the Rye Harbour School, 1915

CHAPTER 2

MRS BESSIE POPE'S (née BOURNE) RECOLLECTIONS

My Father's name was Caesar Bourne and my Mother's was Sarah Ann Upton. My Father was born in Ore and Mother in Lewes. They met on Strand Quay where my Father was unloading a barge of coal for the Gas Works.

They married in Rye Church at 8 o'clock in the morning on April 1st 1901. My sister Susan was born on the 30th September the same year, in a cottage in Little London, between the Queen's Head and the Shop. I was born on 23rd February 1903, over Nan Tucket's Sweet Shop, opposite to Mint House.

A new young Doctor had come to live in Mint House with his wife. He was Dr. Harratt and I was the first baby he delivered in Rye. He looked after us until we moved to Rye Harbour. My Mother never paid him a penny for all his work with us. My three brothers, Stephen, "Caesar" and Thomas, he delivered at Rye Harbour. He and

31

my Dad would settle the pony and trap and he would sit with my Dad drinking tea and chatting, while my poor Mum was working hard with the midwife, who was Mrs Saunders, upstairs. She apparently always had a bad time.

My youngest sister was born on 1st September four years after my brother Tom, in 1912 I think. She was delivered by a new doctor who wouldn't wait and who used forceps, pulling Sally's arm out of its socket. He charged my Mum 7/6, nearly half my Dad's wages at the Chemical Works at that time.

Dad really was a fisherman and did shore jobs when the weather was too bad. Dr Harratt had gone away on a course and the new doctor had to come. I may say, my Mother never forgave Dr. Skinner's assistant, although he stayed in Rye with his family and became quite well known.

I had to start my recollections somewhere. I don't remember when we moved to Rye Harbour, but I must have been very young as I do remember at 2½ following my sister to school and having to be taken home. Apparently I did this every day; in the end the school master said to let me stay. His name was Hatcher and he and his wife taught us. She was a lovely lady and taught me my three R's and knitting, sewing, hem stitching and drawn thread work. Their house was built with the school, so they were always there. We had a lovely Green out in front of the school, where we used to 'drill' and have our play times.

We also had processions to Church on Empire Day, 24th May, after we got a new Vicar. Apparently there hadn't been one in Rye Harbour for some time. He was Reverend Rochford Wade and he Christened me with my three brothers one Easter Sunday. Tom was a baby in long clothes and I remember the smell of narcissus flowers round the font to this day.

Rye Harbour is very different now, but the two shops were still there the last time I was down. The first one was Hedgler's and the Post Office was Watson's. Opposite the Vicarage and up Tram Road was the way to Saunders Farm where we could go with a quart bottle or can and get them filled with milk for tuppence.

The roads were only beach and boulders. We always wore hobnailed boots and they were always dusty. All the houses had wells for water and the Coastguard Houses had coastguards in them with their families. I don't remember all their names, but one family was called Pocock, and their daughter and I were good friends. In the Summer we used to wear rope bottom shoes that cost 6d a pair.

Some families used to go hop-picking, but we never did. I remember the horse drawn wagonnettes used to come early in the morning picking up whole families. There used to be hop gardens where the new estate is now (Tilling Green. Ed.) I believe, at the bottom of Cadboro'.

I do remember when they brought water to Rye Harbour. There was a stand pipe in the middle of the road and people came with kettles and buckets and bedroom jugs to fill up. Eventually they made a tarmac road which was a treat.

We moved to Dover in 1914. I was still going to school - it was funny going to an all girls school, after always sitting next to a boy in class. It was odd too, after having 70-80 pupils and now going to a great big school with about 300 girls, in different classrooms.

Most of the boys I went to school with died in the Lifeboat disaster in 1928.

There used to be a ferry across the Harbour and a tram on the Camber side. People would go to Rye and shop and come home on the Tram and across the Harbour by ferry.

In those days the fishing boats were called smacks. They had no engines, they all sailed. River barges used to take bricks and building material up the Rother to Bodiam.

I remember the Reading Room where my sister and I used to go to the Band of Hope. At Christmas we used to do a play and all the Mums and Dads used to come and see us perform. Once a month we had magic lantern shows.

I can still smell candles and the paraffin in lamps and stoves, and see the man with his horse and cart delivering oil and people's boxes of groceries from the International Stores in Rye.

Today they would say it was not hygienic as all toilets were outside the house.

We had a party on the School Green for the Coronation (1911), with a huge marquee where trestle tables were laid up with all sorts of sandwiches, cake and buns, jellies and fruit, not forgetting tea or lemonade.   We played games and, as a special treat, we were given rides up and down the Harbour Road in the farm wagonnettes - all very exciting! We were each given a mug with King George and Queen Mary on, and the date. Sally was a baby in arms, but was given a mug as well. The day ended with dancing on the Green for the parents. We children were allowed to stay, but when it got dark, the Mums took us home and the Dads went to the pubs. I remember how tired we all were and getting to bed after a lick with a wet flannel instead of our usual nightly wash in front of the fire.

I remember my Mother making us dresses of mauve sateen with very pretty pockets hanging on ribbons. The boys wore black velvet jackets without sleeves and white shirts and grey knickers, all made by hand. How sore my Mum's fingers must have been. I have heard the tale many times of how the velvet jackets were made from her best skirt!   Still we were well turned out for the occasion and she was proud of us.

We always wore white pinny's at school, but I refused to wear one when I was eleven.

Another thing I remember was a large holiday boat on the beach below the Martello Tower.   Students used to come to stay on board during the summer holidays. We kids used to watch them swimming in the sea off Hook Point at the end of the Harbour. They used to play tennis in the Vicarage garden; all so long ago! There weren't many young ladies for them, but enough!

I do recall war breaking out (in 1914).   We were on summer holiday and it was very hot. We were playing five stones on a little bit of green near to the Vicarage fence when someone told us.

The students were sent back to London. There were no factories along the Harbour Road in those days, except the Chemical Works. Troops were brought to camp in the fields with horses to train and to get them used to the noise of gunfire.   We kids used to sit on the fence and watch them.

Another thing I recall was having to learn to sing the French Marseillaise, Sussex by the Sea and the Welsh National song, Land of My Fathers.   There were other patriotic songs we had to learn, but I can't remember them all.   Hearts of Oak I had to sing solo. Ever after at parties, it was my party piece, even when grown up!

At parties everyone had to do something - sing, recite or mime. We entertained ourselves in those days.

One day a huge yacht came into Rye Harbour with Sir Algernon Guinness looking for recruits, as his ship had been taken over by the Government for war work. My Dad joined him; and for the first time in his life, had to wear a collar and tie with his uniform. He looked very smart.

None of the other fishermen went. Dad and the yacht were sent to Dover, where a gun was fitted to the boat and then they were used to transport food across the Channel to France for the troops.

That is why we moved to Dover in early 1915. We went by train and the furniture by Wright and Pankhurst's horse and waggon. We were there about six months when Dad told Mum that they had been posted to Southampton, so we need never have moved!

Anyway, to get back to Rye Harbour, between the Coastguard Lookout and the 'William the Conqueror' was a lovely bungalow in which old Mrs Downey lived, and we lived in a cottage behind the pub. When I was big enough, she used to give me 6d a week for cleaning her step, running errands, cleaning knives on an emery board etc. She also had a pet jackdaw that one day stood on my head and pecked my forehead. The whole of Rye Harbour heard my screams, believe me, and I didn't go to school that day. The scar is still there.

My sister Susan was much bigger than me and much more clever. She won a scholarship for the Grammar School, but refused to go, so left school at 13. She went to work as a between maid in a big house on the Camber Tram side.

My favourite memory is of seeing all the fishing boats coming down the river out to sea in full sail. We all used to stand on the pier and wave. They would be gone for weeks, landing their fish at Folkestone, Hastings or Newhaven, whichever market they were nearest to. The ship owners would come on Saturday afternoons and give the wives some money for weekend shopping. When the boats came home, they would have a settlement meeting and each man got his fair share. We would be quite well off for a few days and go with sixpence and get eggs for all the family on Sunday morning for breakfast, fresh from the nests.

I can see the men and boys in punts picking mussels off the Harbour walls. My Mum would cook them in a boiler over the fire and then get them out of their shells. She then put them in jars covered with vinegar - very tasty!

I remember the Harbour Road was flints and men would sit on the road side breaking stones to fill up the holes in the road.

I recall seeing my first motor car driven by Dr. Ticehurst and his wife, bringing Sally home from Hastings Hospital where she had been for 10 months in his care. She even went to his wedding, dressed 'to kill' by the nurses. In those days the Hospital was where the White Rock Theatre is now, and she was one of the first children to have x-ray treatment, but they could never put her arm back in its socket. She never made any trouble of it at all though!

There was no public transport in those days - you walked or begged a lift from the baker or anyone with a horse and cart. Sometimes we were lucky!

We had to go to Sunday School in the morning, Church in the evening.

I dimly remember the maroon going off and everyone rushing out of Church with the lifeboat men, to stand on the beach and watch the rescue, Everyone lent a hand and we kids got in the way. Whoever was free went into the lifeboat. As I recall they were mostly fishermen, but it would always be fully manned and they were all volunteers.

Another silly thing I remember is what we used to say what Rye Church bells were saying. In the Summer, a gang of us would go up to Rye Church Sunday morning service. We could hear the bells on our way, "Why don't you leave my wife alone? She is so drunk, she can't get home." I doubt if one would hear them now with present day traffic!

In 1928 I lived in South Undercliff in Rye, next door to Grace Wilkinson, who was about to have her first child (Harry). Her sister's husband was drowned in the lifeboat disaster. I walked down to Rye Harbour in dreadful weather with Grace when we heard about it. I stayed with her sister until after the funeral. It was very moving - all the coffins were in the Harbour Road and we processed to the Churchyard behind them.

CHAPTER 3

AN ACCOUNT OF A HOLIDAY IN JULY 1905.

(This letter of 31st July 1905 was reproduced in the Parish Magazine in December 1980.)

Dear Mr Paine,

Knowing how interested you are in nautical matters, I thought you would like to hear how I spent my holiday this year.

I went for a fortnight on one of the fishing smacks, a Rye trawler called the 'Fancy'. She was cutter rigged, about 20 tons and belonged to a Mr Kingsnorth Reeves, a big pot in Rye.

The crew consisted of three men, the skipper, named John Ford, Elgar Gladwish or 'Shinner' and Jack Roberts, otherwise 'Rats'.

The skipper was about sixty years old and had been at sea ever since he was ten years old. He used to work on a Lowestoft boat.

Old 'Shinner' was the same age as the skipper, but he had worked principally on coasting barges. He was a lazy old beast and was supposed to be a teetotaller, but he used to get half drunk every time we came ashore on cider and ginger wine. He and the skipper had a terrible row one day and the skipper gave him the sack.

Jack was the one I liked best. He had been all manner of things and had been all over the world. He told me he was first apprenticed to a sailmaker, but left that and went to sea in a four master to Australia. There he worked on a sheep farm near Ballarat, but did not stop at it long as it was too lonely for him. He said sometimes, for weeks at a time, his only companions were a horse and a dog and his nearest neighbour was twenty miles away.

He then went to sea again and travelled to New Zealand, America, South Africa and to China. He was fourteen years at sea in these big boats and when he came back to England, he went with Sanger's Circus as a tent repairer. He and the blacksmith used to sleep in a cart. From Sangers he went back to sea and worked on the trawlers. He was a jolly chap and could tell some fine yarns about the different places he had seen and about the boats he had been on.

We used generally to fish in Rye Bay and, our boat being a trawler, we chiefly caught flat fish and very little of that. They say that the grounds are becoming exhausted and I don't wonder. It is only a mile and a half wide and about four miles long and very often there were thirty or forty boats sweeping the grounds at once.

As perhaps you know, the boats fish on the flood as the fish come up to meet the tide for food. It is a fine sight when the trawl is hauled in and they open the net, the fish come down with a bang and go all over the deck. We caught a big conger one day, about six feet long and as thick as my thigh. It only fetched 4/9d though. We had a steam capstan for hauling in the trawl and anchor. They are filthy things and cover everything with black bits ('blacks').

Of course, it is a very rough life and I found it a bit "off" at first, but soon got used to it. The bunks are just shelves with no blankets and only the skipper has a mattress, but I preferred the boards to that. You turn in with all your clothes on, boots and all, and sleep like a top. The cabin was an awf ul place and I should think the temperature was never less than 80°F. What with the galley fire and the 'huffy' as they called the capstan, the heat is almost unbearable.

Jack used to do the cooking and very well he did it, though it was a bit different to what I had been used to.   Everything is boiled in the same pot, potatoes, meat, cabbage and plum duff, and is served up in basins which are stuck on the floor. You carve off what you like and when you have done, the correct thing is to wipe your knife and fork, (if you have a fork), on your trousers and then jam it up in the beams. The water that the grub is boiled in is not wasted as, when it is salted and peppered, it forms the most delightful drink, at least so they said, but I did not tackle it, a look was sufficient for me!   Jack was a very ingenious chap and made a novel fish slice. He bored a number of holes in a scollop shell and then lashed a small wooden handle to It. it worked fine.

Nothing very startling happened while I was on the boat, but one night we had a terrible storm.   We had to take in two reefs in the mains'l and take in the tops'l, which jammed and would not come down till Elgar went aloft and cleared it. It was rather exciting, and then lightning lit up the sea for miles, as clear as day.

Another time we lost nearly all our gear. It appears that there is a steamer called the 'Panto' sunk right in the middle of the fishing grounds - it has been down about two years now.   Being a misty night, we could not see the 'Ness' light and take any bearings and so we trawled right down on this steamer. We tore all our net, which was a new one, and cut one of our braces. For a time we hung on one thin rope and were very lucky to get away with any of our gear. They say there are hundreds of pounds worth of gear down on the 'Panto', but they don't want to have her blown up as it would make matters worse, as she is in one lump at present. I saw two boats lose their gear while I was out.

We often fished right out in the traffic and sometimes, of a night, big sailers would bear right down on us, until the skipper waved a deck light and then they would sheer off not twenty yards away. They looked fine, sometimes having every sail set.

One night one of the fleet got mixed up in a mackerel - men's net. It was a calm night and we laid about a mile away, but we could hear every word they said. The language .... , cabmen are not in it!

I saw a good many big liners while I was out and we passed a fleet of torpedo boats and cruisers one morning. One day we passed a sailer called the 'Mengozin Sophie Charlotte' of Bremen, being towed by a tug. She is about the largest sailer I have seen. French fishing boats used to be fairly numerous.

I think this holiday has been one of the most interesting I have had. The men never minded being questioned and would explain everything I did not understand. Jack taught me to drive the capstan. Old Shinner used to give me sailing lessons and, in my second week, I often took a spell at the tiller and could put the old lady about myself single-handed, though you have to be careful. The sails seem made of iron and, when you take them in, you break all your nails.

It was almost impossible to get a good wash on board as fresh water is at a premium and salt is no good. What with 'huffy' blacks and being sunburnt, I looked a regular nigger, but the trip did me good and I felt ready to fight anybody when I came home.

I could not have gone with nicer men and, considering I had never seen them before, I think I was very lucky. None, or very few of these smackmen ever take any beer or spirits on board with them, though they have plenty of both when they are ashore. Their chief drink at sea is tea, which is made in a kettle and they drink gallons of this. I never saw a spirit or beer bottle all the time I was on the

'Fancy'.

The crew have no fixed screw but work on commission. It is worked like this. From their total earnings, all living expenses, cost of coal, water etc. are deducted and what remains is divided into 5¾ shares. The owner takes 2½, the skipper 1¼, and the two men have a share a piece. Our total earnings for three weeks only mounted to £23 odd and Jack's share worked out to £3.6.7., which was very bad.

We fished up last Friday week and came into Rye at 10.30pm. It was a fine moonlight night and the Harbour looked very pretty. Saturday morning we went up to the town to the Ypres Castle Inn, they call it the 'Wipers', and had the settling up and I came back to Hastings by train.

I think I have told you the whole yarn and hoping it has not bored you!

It it sad that the signature is missing from this wonderful account. We do know that, in 1905, the writer lived at 12 Cambridge Gardens, Hastings.

Fishing Boats on the Rother at Rye Harbour looking across to the Harbour Master's Office

CHAPTER 4

MEMORIES FROM THE CHURCH MAGAZINE
AUGUST 1913 : by G. JAMES
(kindly contributed by Miss Ena Saunders)

Leaving London via London Bridge Railway Station, we were on our way to camp at Rye. A lady at the Church had paid for me and, with my short haircut and kitbag, my mother had seen me off. I was nine years old.

This was a great adventure and my first time away from home. The Vicar (Dinge) was afterwards to marry me, seventeen years away.

When we arrived at Rye Town Station, some of the boys who had been before told me of a short cut to the Harbour where the camp was, so, following them, we went off along the railway line that led us to the Harbour. It was four miles away and took us over an hour to walk. We came to the Laundry first, then the smelly Chemical Works which did things to coal mostly and, after that we could see the Church laying back from the road near the School. When we got to the village we had to walk across the shingle and, at last, we were there. If ours was the short way, I wondered why everybody was there before us!

Very tired and hungry, we all sat down in the marquee to tea and bread and jam. After tea we filled our palliasses with straw and were told where we were to sleep. I was in a bunk that was close to the ceiling of the corrugated iron hut. The roof was not fixed down so one end could be raised for ventilation. We all had two blankets, and no sheets, of course.

As it grew darker we had our supper - cocoa and bread and butter - then prayers and bed. When we awoke it was Sunday morning and soon we would be off to Church in the village. We washed by filling bowls with cold water from the tanks and, after washing, had breakfast. This was enamel mugs of tea, a boiled egg, and plenty of bread and butter.

Our hut was detailed to clear up the marquee after breakfast and others had different jobs.

Soon we were over the shingle to Church. With the village people we nearly filled the Church, so I sat at the back so I could get out first. Father St John was a great tall man, over six feet in height, and he conducted the service as the Vicar of Rye Harbour was on holiday. Mitty Mit sat at the back near me to see the boys did not misbehave. Mitty Mit was a dwarf who worked in our parish of St Paul's without pay for many years. I think the camping ground and the tin huts which were used each summer belonged to him. As the years passed, I grew to like him more, but I hardly knew him then and he used to call me Jameoh. I was as tall as he and sat quiet as a mouse in the back row.

Some of the boys with good voices were up in the front. Before we came away to camp Dinge had had me go to choir practice to try my voice for the choir. When Mr Bottle had asked me to sing a scale they all looked at me as though I made a rude noise. Dinge smiled and said 'his voice has already broken,' so I was no use to the choir.

We went back to camp after Church, where the lady who was the cook had prepared a lovely meal. Her name was Mrs Smith and she was a marvel with the the cooking things she had. She made lovely suet puddings in cloths which she boiled in the copper in the open - her fisherman husband would stoke the fire for hours with odd bits of wood.

We were told beforehand that no one was allowed to bathe unless one of the older ones were present, so we hoped we could bathe after dinner. No such luck, so we spent the afternoon finding out about the place. At the back of the camp on the sea side was a big dyke used for drainage and, between that and the camp, was the lavatory. This was three long wooden scaffold poles arranged over a trench and hessian cloths fixed around it.

The camp consisted of five huts for sleeping and for cooking, and two marquees, one for a Chapel and one to eat in. These were hired from Gassons of Rye and, in later years, when we had a large number of people down there, we hired old Army bell tents as well. We bought sweets at the village shop which was run by Mr Black, a dragon of a man with piercing eyes who had been a policeman in the Colonial Service. Mr Cutting ran the ferry and it cost halfpenny to cross. Near the ferry was the Coastguard Station and a pub, the

'William the Conqueror'. On the shingle in front of the Coastguard Station stood a boat, the Blue House boat used by poor boys as a holiday home and supported by Cambridge House.

There was so much to look at and find out about. Dinge promised to take us down to the sea to bathe after tea. So after tea we went off to bathe. No one used bathing costumes, not even Mitty Mit and Dinge. I couldn't swim that much, but that first time swimming without anything on was lovely. The coast here was bad for swimming - really deep shelves and shingle; also strong currents in and out of the Harbour made it difficult for poor swimmers, There is always a wind blowing and sometimes, if the wind was strong, it made big waves and it was difficult to get in and out.

Dinge and Mitty Mit kept watch while we were playing in the water and, when we were all drying, they would go in singing and splashing about for a little while. The bathing place was quite a way from the camp and us boys would search the coarse shamrock-like vegetation for all kinds of things - small crabs were in the ditches that criss-crossed all this area that is sometimes covered by the sea.

About the middle of the week, we were coming back from the bathe along the Harbour when we saw Father Churchward coming towards us. He told Father St John that he had been accepted for the Mission Field (UMCA); then he said 'I must have a swim' and started to undress. 'No Churchward, not here, it is dangerous in the Harbour', but, saying 'I only want a dip', he was in. We all waited as he fought against the current that was dragging him out into the middle of the Harbour. Father St John hurried down to the edge and we all stood and waited to see what would happen. Fear was very real and I imagined Father Churchward being swept right out to sea and being drowned. After a long time Father Churchward made it back to the edge and got out exhausted. Dinge looked round at us and said angrily, 'now you know why we are strict about bathing.' What a lesson! The U. M. C. A. nearly lost a missionary.

AUGUST 1913 :THE CONTINUING STORY OF RYE HOLIDAYS

The cricket pitch was very short because we played on the only hard and flat piece of ground near the huts. When we hit the tennis ball, it was stopped by the slopes of shingle that surrounded the camp. Water was brought to the camp by a boy from the village carrying two buckets with a yoke that fitted on his shoulders. Years after we still called him 'Buckets', even when he was in the lifeboat crew.

When we arrived on the first day, it was considered an honour to be the first boy to make for Camber Castle and climb the worn stairs to where the first floor used to be, and walk round the inside on the supports that were still left. I never tried it - it was too frightening even watching, for the fall was about twenty feet to the rough ground below.

On the way to Camber Castle we passed the Black House which was owned by a man and woman who had been on the stage - and when we went there for teas, we saw many things of the theatre and photos of actors and actresses cut out and stuck on the walls.

Mr Saunders would take the Vicar to town in a brougham pulled by a farm horse to buy or shop, but most things were brought from the village. Mitty Mit would lead us in singing songs with his cracked voice when it got too dark to play games, and then supper - cocoa and bread and jam and into bed.

Sometime during the first week, the tea at one of the meals would taste funny and the next day the toilet was well patronised. I found out many years after that the Vicar put liquid cascara in the tea once in the first week and once in the second.

Over the ferry at the Harbour was a railway that ran from the golf course at Camber Sands to Rye Town by the Salts just below the Landgate and Gun Garden. This train was very small, run on coal, and was called Puffing Billy. It was very cheap and we boys used to use it when going to town and our money hadn't run out.

Our camp was on the way to the Lifeboat House from the village, so if the rocket went off to call the men and women to launch the boat, either for practice or rescue, the village people came past the camp, so we, or most of us, would follow to help the launch. It meant pulling and pushing the lifeboat over the shingle on boards to the water's edge and then pulling her out with special tackle anchored out at sea. I have helped in many a launch and always I was impressed with the eager volunteering if they were short of a man. The Rye Lifeboat never had an engine, only sails and oars. It was housed in its lifeboat house on a very bleak and lonely stretch of coast about a mile and a half from the village, and the only time we could get in to look around was when a launch was being made. It was then an untidy jumble of strange gear and tackle, mixed up with clothes and rope as the men fought to get the boat out.

At last the boat would slide gently into the sea and those who were left were the women with anxious faces and shawls, the older men and us boys, only just realising how serious a business this was. That night after supper when prayers were taken by Dinge, who always prayed for the lifeboat men, we thought a lot about the scene at the lifeboat station.

Many cases of sunburn occurred and, after a hot day playing on the shingle slopes, the back of the dyke, and the many activities that went on, many groans could be heard before we went to sleep. I think the rough blankets did not help!

On the last day at camp the marquees had to be struck and packed ready to go back to Gassons. On the Saturday after the two weeks, we made our way to Rye to board the train back home. My mother, along with a lot more mums, was waiting at the station to greet us, and listen to the many accounts of what had gone on.

Rye Harbour Church in the snow

CHAPTER 5

MEMORIES OF GLADYS MORPHY (née FIRRELL)

I lived in Rye Harbour, a small village of about one hundred houses, not far from the town of Rye, where I was born in 1916. I am the second child of Nancy and Tom Firrell and have a sister Nancy, who is fourteen months older, and a brother Tom, who is three and a half years younger than myself. My mother came from the village of Ore near Hastings and my father was brought up in Rye, where he was born, with his one brother and five sisters. My parents were married in Rye Church, as I myself was in 1939, to Edward Morphy of Rye.

When I was a young girl we lived at 2, Inkerman Row. It had two bedrooms, sitting room, kitchen and scullery, as it was then called, which contained a built-in copper and sink with a cold water tap. Outside was a flush toilet and coal house. We had a dog and kept bantams. My father worked nearby driving a small train to and from the seashore. Men working on the shore loaded blue boulders into trugs suspended from yokes on their shoulders. They carried these to skips on the train. The boulders were sent to factories in other parts of the country to be used in glazing china. My aunt and sister-in-law also worked at collecting boulders for which they were paid 4d. a skip.

My father also did running repairs to the engine and to any other machinery that went wrong. The loco also brought in stones from the seashore to a crushing plant in the Harbour.

We saw very little of our father apart from mealtimes and he would very often be called out at night to repair machinery and still have to be at work at six the following morning. Some nights he did not get home until very late and we would listen out on the dark stormy nights for the sound of the little train coming home as there were no street lights to see by.

In the house we had lamps that hung from the ceiling that were filled with paraffin, and a stove that burnt coal. My father always chopped enough wood at weekends to last the week, as he had to light the fire in the morning to get the kettle to boil before he had a cup of tea. He also cleaned all our shoes.

My father was a great one for work as he also had an allotment garden which grew vegetables, some of which would last us all the winter. Carrots were put into sand to keep and onions tied up in the shed. Greens were grown all year round. He also loved growing sweet peas and I well remember gathering them with my brother and sister. He also kept pigs and it was a great occasion when one was killed. A butcher from Rye, Mr Larkin, came to kill the pig and all the village would come to watch and of course have some meat when it was cut up. I remember being very upset and afraid and wouldn't eat any of it, but I think I did, as I was told that it was something else. My brother, I am told, managed to fall out of his pram into a bowl of pig fat. My father loved "fleed cakes" that were made from the fat.

My father also sent away for fishing nets which required mending and he would mend them with a special needle. He traded in my mother's maiden name as Hilder and Co. As a child, I would take them across the road to the shop which was also the Post Office where they would be weighed and sent back, I believe, to Grimsby.

We always had a car. One I remember was a Ford which had side pieces to be put on if it had rained. The roof would go up first and the sides clipped on afterwards. We would sometimes go to Sidley to see my father's sister or my mother's sister at Ore.

We often got home to find a young lad from Rye called Charlie Tiltman already indoors with the lamp alight, especially if there had been a storm. The lads of the village always watched my father repair the car. We had several types, I remember a Studebaker and a Morris with a 'Dickie' seat. A Ford was kept in a galvanized garage built by my father. One day, after a storm, he looked out of the window and said to my mother that someone must have had a night out in an old car as there it was, standing there. He then realised that it was his car and the garage, that had no doors, had blown away in the storm.

As children we would love to be able to go out after tea, but we were not allowed to if it was dark, except when the Slate Club had to be paid. We would take the money to the Sailor's Home where my friend's father and Mr Pope would take it. I believe it was shared out at Christmas and would help to buy presents and extra food.

The Sailor's Home was in rooms in the upstairs of a large house. The house was looked after by a Mrs Mesher and her family and the rooms kept ready in case any ships were wrecked. Downstairs was a billiard room where the men from the village could go and there was also a reading room.

Next door was the Church Hall where they held Mother's Meetings, concerts and where the Church Army would come and give a service. This we loved and had a good time running wild before the meeting started. We would sing "B.I.B.L.E. - That's The Book For Me" and there would be big black hearts and big red hearts displayed. When it finished, instead of going straight home, we loved to get together and tie the doorknobs of two houses together, knock on the doors and run away. On Bonfire Night the boys would let off squibs in the Gent's toilet because they sounded louder.

We had to make our own fun and, after school, I would go out sketching boats, the Church and other views. Every year artists came to stay and, of course, we would watch them and draw the same things. I would also take my tea out to the Martello Tower with a friend and we would see who could eat the most. We would also darn socks using a tennis ball to fill the hole and would see who could be the neatest. There were no socks that didn't go in holes in those days! Other times we played in my friend's shed with our dolls and once a year she had a party for her birthday, which was great fun, as no one else in the village was well enough off to afford one.

When my mother's brother John came back from Canada, he bought us a crystal set with ear phones. Later on we had a cabinet gramophone which had to be wound up. No one had holidays, just Easter Monday and Christmas.

We always went to Sunday School and to Church. The Vicar's daughter took us for Guides each week in the Mission Room which was next door to the Post Office. Once a year the British Legion gave a concert there and, when I was older, I went there for social evenings. They also used the hall for dances and wedding receptions. On the day of a wedding people put up flags from bedroom windows and, if anyone died, the whole village would pull their curtains. Dan Maskell was married at the Church as they were staying at the Vicarage. The Vicar and his wife were very nice and friendly and the

Vicar's wife took the Mothers' Meeting once a week in the Church Room.

During the Summer we played hopscotch and skipping and spun tops. We picked blackberries and sold a dish of them to Mrs Fowler who took in lodgers in the holidays. We had six weeks holiday from school and a few people from the village went hop-picking at Icklesham.

Most of the men were fishermen, catching plaice, dabs and skate and I remember my mother cooking fish after the boats had come in and we were called downstairs to have some. At mackerel time we were allowed to go down to the seashore to get them from the nets.

On Saturdays there were always jobs to be done, cleaning knives on a board, spoons and forks, and sometimes the kitchen to scrub. There was always a lot to be done in the home. There were no carpets, only rugs and so lino had to be scrubbed and polished, the cooker had to have flues cleaned out each week and the stove black-leaded. It used to take all of one day to do the washing. The rubbish was saved to heat the copper which the washing was boiled in. The whites were blued in the rinsed water and, the next day, you did the ironing which took ages as the old flat iron was heated on the stove and took a long time to get hot enough. There was always enough food left over from Sunday to fry up for Monday as there wasn't time to cook. My parents bought a primus and so we were able to get a cup of tea quicker. We had electricity brought to the village in the thirties and we were then able to have a cooker and kettle and no longer had to fill the paraffin lamps.

During the summer I remember cheap jacks displaying their wares in the field over the road from our house, and the people would come to buy china and other goods from them. We lived next door to a sweet and vegetable shop which sold off specked oranges, four for a penny. They were lovely - only the peel had gone off.

We went to school in the village. We had three teachers, infant, junior and senior and the room was divided up, one half for the infants and juniors and the other half for the seniors. We were taught to read, write, do arithmetic, to draw, history, geography, needle work, basketwork, and the boys did wood work. We made children's dresses with smocking and dresses for ourselves. The school went up to Standard 7 and there were only a few boys and girls and later they had to go to the Senior School in Rye. My brother went there and he and his friend had to walk the two miles there and back. We left school at 14 in those days.

There were no buses in the village and I remember my father running people to Rye in his Ford. Later a firm called Wright and Pankhurst sent a bus once a week. The milkman came from Rye with his horse and cart and Mr Long, the Rye baker, also called.

Some children of the village used to wear rope slippers in the summer and I always wished I could have some as well. They used to have broken biscuits instead of cake for tea and we used to think they were lucky. They also had a little sister in the Churchyard and used to put flowers on the grave. I used to wish we had someone we could put flowers on for as well.

My mother used to make our dresses. She was very good at sewing and knitting and did a lot of it. She was also a very good cook. No one went very far and didn't go out of the village much unless to visit the doctor. No one went on holiday but we were lucky we had a car.

Dutch and German ships often came to Rye Harbour. The German ships brought in timber and one ship seemed to belong to a family who brought their sister along as well. They sometimes came to our village socials, very smartly dressed. The Dutch ships came to dredge the mouth of the Harbour and the crews would come to the shop to buy fruit and vegetables. I remember the sea coming over the sea wall at Winchelsea and it flooded all around the houses. Later a new sea wall was built.

It was a very sad time when the lifeboat capsized and all the crew drowned. My father, who was working on the seashore, saw it capsize and sent his mate off on the other train to tell the coastguards who said that it was coming round to come into Harbour but, of course, it wasn't as they soon realised. It was a dreadful morning; never have I known one like it. The lifeboatmen had to battle their way to the shore to launch the lifeboat as it was kept on the beach over a mile away and they had to run all the way. I remember the funeral well.

In 1929 we moved to 3, Stonework Cottage and later to the Tram

Road. We moved from the Harbour in about 1936 and lived in New Winchelsea Road, Rye. My childhood was very happy but my mother never had very good health and I stayed at home to look after her until I married in 1939. After the war we settled in Fleet, Hampshire and my husband was Head of Science at Basingstoke School for many years.

We are very grateful to Mrs Deborah Broadley, the daughter of Mrs Morphy (née Firrell), for sending this recollection from Fleet, Hampshire.

The Rye Harbour Lighthouse, demolished c.1963

CHAPTER 6

SCHOOLDAYS AT RYE HARBOUR SCHOOL
by MISS ENA SAUNDERS

When I was young all the village children went to the little school near the Church. It was a Church School and, once or twice a week, the Vicar gave us religious instruction. On the Saints' Days we went to Church for a service, and there was a Sunday School for the younger children and a Bible Class for the older ones. We also had our Band of Hope, and some of the older members won a prize in the Hastings Music Festival. As you can imagine they were extremely proud of this achievement. Our teacher was Miss Whitlock, daughter of Rye's Chief Inspector of Police, and she had bright auburn hair.

Our school had three classrooms and two fairly large cloakrooms, and we had two playgrounds and a large grass field front and back. The boys played football on the front field, and the girls played netball at the back of the school.

The school finally closed just before the outbreak of war, and for a number of years it was reduced to a very dilapidated state. As everyone knows, it has now been restored and made into three very attractive homes.

We were taught to study the weather, and every morning had to report in our books the direction and strength of the wind, the cloud conditions, and whether it was wet or dry.

Every day our hands, hair and our shoes were inspected.

During the summer months, we were taken for nature walks in the fields and shown the birds and flowers and, when these coincided with practice launching of the lifeboat, we all loved it. Winding the boat in and pulling the sleepers up was a great excitement. The sleepers were well greased and placed a certain distance apart, for the boat to get over the beach.

Each Good Friday a group of us girls (about twelve years old) were taken to the woods to pick primroses to decorate the Church for Easter Sunday. We had a lovely time rambling in the woods and walked both ways to Udimore and back; Mrs Mills always took us.

(She was Mrs Doris Cutting's mother). At this time in my life about half the population were related to one another, aunts, uncles and cousins, but this is all changed now.

My schooldays were very happy, although at one time I had to teach the Juniors because we were short of teachers, and I did not like this at all.

"I always enjoyed playing Tally Ho on the front field at School on frosty mornings and I loved country dance class."

The Coastguard Station was fully manned by coastguards and their families until 1923 when it closed. We were very sorry to see our friends leaving Rye Harbour.

Quite a large group of us were Confirmed in 1922 when the Reverend Walter March was here.

At home I was busy on the farm feeding the newly hatched chicks and ducks and I always had my own pet lamb.

CHILDREN OF RYE HARBOUR : 1928.

CHAPTER 7

SCRIPT AS RECORDED

THE RYE HARBOUR LIFEBOAT DISASTER

*The story of this lifeboat, lost with all hands on November 15th 1928, told
by the people of Rye Harbour.
Compiled and narrated by John Sharp
Produced by Anthony Thwaite.*
TRANSMISSION : HOME SERVICE IN SOUTH EAST
Monday 17th November 1958, 6.35-7.00pm
RECORDED: 11th November 1958

THE MARY STANFORD LIFEBOAT DISASTER

1. ANNOUNCER:

Thirty years ago last Thursday, the Rye Harbour Lifeboat 'THE
MARY STANFORD', was lost with all hands. This programme is not
a debate or inquest on the disaster; all such matters were dealt with in
the Coroners' Courts and at the official Board of Trade Enquiry. This
is a tribute to those men of Rye Harbour, and is told by people who
still live in that district - people who cannot forget that day. Here is
John Sharp, who begins the story.

2. JOHN SHARP:

Early in the morning, on the 15th November 1928, Rye Harbour
Lifeboat, 'The Mary Stanford', was launched in order to assist the
'Alice', a small Latvian vessel in difficulty off Dungeness. The
weather conditions were among the worst in living memory. Frank
Saunders was a launcher.

3. FRANK SAUNDERS:

It was a very dark and wild morning when we went to launch -
blowing pretty well a full gale from the South South-East.

4. JOHN SHARP:

George Mills was the signalman.

5. GEORGE MILLS:

On the morning of the 15th November I heard a maroon fired
about 5 o'clock in the morning. It was blowing a very heavy gale of
wind and was very pitch dark.

6. JOHN SHARP:

Jimmy Downey had been cox'n of the Rye Harbour Lifeboat for 17 years, and for a very long time a member of her crew. At the time of the disaster he had been out of the Lifeboat for some time, but he helped to launch her that morning.

7. JIMMY DOWNEY:

When it come this morning she was called, I went up there and I helped launch, and it was a most shocking day. One of the worst I've ever experienced, I think really, and I've experienced a good many rough days and been in the lifeboat in some rough times; but that was a bad time.

8. JOHN SHARP:

Over at Pett Level, Reg Cooke was in charge of the Life Saving Apparatus Team, and indeed he still is. Although he had nothing whatever to do with the Rye Harbour Lifeboat, he well remembers the weather.

9. REG COOKE:

Well, I don't think that I've ever seen as much sea in Rye Bay as there was that morning. You couldn't see across the marsh because of the spray from the water. It wasn't fog, it was just the spray off the shallow breaking water. It was a dead short tide. What I mean by that is that it was a neap tide. And that made the water worse in the Bay than it normally would have been. It even browned the trees on the weather side for three or four miles inland. It was only due to the sea blowing the salt mist on to them. But it really was rough, there's no doubt about that. I don't think - and I'm pretty sure of it - that I've never seen anything like it in Rye Harbour in my life before or since. I've seen it very nearly approaching it - the day the Hastings Lifeboat capsized was pretty nearly as bad - but not quite.

10. JOHN SHARP:

Mr. Mitchell was at sea serving with the Home Fleet.

11. MR MITCHELL:

On the night of the disaster I myself was at sea serving in one of His Majesty's ships exercising the Home Fleet, and the gale that was blowing at the time, even out there, which was quite some distance from the South coast as you can all imagine; as far as my recollections take me, the gale was about Force 9 to 12.

12. JOHN SHARP:

If that weather is remembered by a man who was serving in a big vessel, think of the cox'n and crew and the launchers of 'The Mary Stanford', trying to get her afloat. It was low water, and that didn't help.

13. FRANK SAUNDERS:

We had very great difficulty in launching the boat. It happened to be a low-water launch, and we had a long stretch of sand to pull the boat across before we could get her afloat, and it did seem that the boat didn't want to go that morning, 'cos I think we pulled her into the water three times before she really got afloat. She knocked back with the sea the first couple of times before she really got away with it.

14. JOHN SHARP:

Dennis Cutting was a launcher.

15. DENNIS CUTTING:

Well, I lost three brothers and a brother-in-law in this lifeboat disaster and I was on the end of the rope launching her that morning, and it was very rough, and - well - I think everyone done the best they possibly could. I don't think the boat would ever have got off if the crew hadn't got out and helped to launch her. And as we was launching her, the sea broke right over our heads - well, everyone were wet through including the crew, before they got aboard the boat.

16. JOHN SHARP:

Jack Saunders, Frank's brother, was another launcher.

17. JACK SAUNDERS:

The boat was launched and I was surfman, which acted in case anyone was knocked out of the boat, I was on the beach with a lifejacket on with two men always on a line, so that, in case a man was knocked over, my job was to run in and get hold of him and they'd haul us ashore.

18. JOHN SHARP:

A further trouble which these men had to put up with was the tidy step from village to boathouse.

19. FRANK SAUNDERS:

It was blowing a full gale, and of course you realise the distance we had to travel before we reached the boathouse, across rough shingle and fields, fences, obstacles of various kinds in the pitch dark, a journey of approximately a mile and a half from the village to the boathouse, and I don't suppose, unless anyone knows this coast, the difficulties of launching a lifeboat by manpower across this type of shore; being so very flat, it's entirely in contrast to many lifeboat stations where the boats are launched from a slipway. I'd like to emphasise that this boat had to be pulled by the launchers and crew themselves. We had to pull it, as I said, across approximately a hundred yards of beach, and equally the same distance across flat sand, walking into the water until we got deep enough for the boat to float. This meant some of our launchers - the foremost launchers on the ropes - had to be in water up round their shoulders.

20. JOHN SHARP:

Mrs. Newton, widow of the Rev. Harry Newton who was the Vicar of Rye Harbour, saw the men battle against the wind on their way to the launching.

21. MRS NEWTON:

We all went to bed at the Vicarage feeling very upset, hoping against all hope that the boat would not be fetched out, but knowing the storm and the violence of it, we felt sure it would be. When the maroon went off, my husband immediately jumped out of bed, switched on the light, the curtains were drawn back, and almost before one could think, those lifeboat men were running round the Vicarage on to the boat. We didn't know how they did it, in fact, the Vicar said it seemed almost as though they had slept with their clothes on they were there so quickly; and they called up to the Vicar, they could see him dressing, and they said "It's no good, Sir, you can't do it, we are having to bend double." We looked through the window and the lights from the Vicarage shone on the men as they went. It was a remarkable sight, they were drenched before they got to the Vicarage and of course as they went on they got wetter and wetter and they were walking completely double.

22. JOHN SHARP:

On a morning when you or I wouldn't want to poke even our noses round the back door, those people never heard of the word 'hesitation'.

23. JACK SAUNDERS:

One thing I would like to mention was the cox'n himself didn't know what was happening, what they was going for, which normally he was always told when the maroon fired. When he got there he asked the Secretary what was on; he said, "well there's this collision eight miles South - West of Dungeness and the lifeboat's wanted"; so he said, "We'll go" - he didn't hesitate.

24. JOHN SHARP:

They never had dawdled at Rye Harbour when that lifeboat was needed.

25. JIMMY DOWNEY:

When there was bad times and the old gun used to go off, I noticed as many as sixty launchers besides crew, when it has been low water time. Never turned anybody away: "get the boat off, get her off. She's called; get her off as quick as you can."

26. JOHN SHARP:

And get her off they did.

27. FRANK SAUNDERS:

She'd only been afloat a matter of seconds, I think it could have been, when a message came recalling the boat, services no longer required. The signalman, Mr. Mills, fired his recall signal and I myself ran across the sands, ran into the water to try and attract the attention of the crew, but of course the weather was very very bad, and they were too occupied in getting the sails set. I don't think they ever saw my signal.

28. JOHN SHARP:

"Getting the sails set." Remember that 'The Mary Stanford' was a pulling and sailing type lifeboat. She had no engines and no radio and none of the devices which today we regard as commonplace. She was a non-self-righting surf-boat, suitable for the local conditions, and there were several of her type in use at that time. With a fifteen-foot oar in their hands and sails to set in a gale of wind, it is small wonder that those men never saw the recall signal. The spray and the rain were as thick as Stockholm Tar, but George Mills the signalman did his best.

29. GEORGE MILLS:

And as the boat was afloat I stepped on to the edge of the water everything was all right, and when I made my way back again to the boathouse one of the coastguards came and met me, and asked me to fire a recall signal as the boat crew were saved. So I fired one Verey light, but owing to the bad weather, the people in the boat were looking ahead, they couldn't see my signal, so I fired two more, and after that of course the boat was out of sight owing to the weather.

30. JOHN SHARP:

What happened to 'The Mary Stanford' between her being launched and her capsizing we shall never know, because none of the crew lived to tell the tale. What we do know, however, is that seventeen men spent several hours in Rye Bay under weather conditions which worsened when daylight came - and they were looking for men who weren't there. The crew of the 'Alice' had already been rescued by the German steamer 'Smyrna'. Eventually 'The Mary Stanford' made for home, but for those seventeen fishermen there was no homecoming. Cecil Marchant of Camber, then a boy of fifteen, actually saw her capsize.

31. CECIL MARCHANT:

Well, I was walking along the sands on this particular morning, and it was a very rough and wild morning, and I was out looking for driftwood; I'd a gun with me, if there was any stray ducks about I was going to have them. I knew the lifeboat had been launched, I had heard that. I wasn't very old, about fifteen at the time, and I was looking about to sea, the tide was about three parts in. I started on my way back home and I just turned round to have another look at the sea to see if anything was being washed up, as I usually did, the sky happened to clear and I saw a boat.

I watched it for only a matter of seconds, I suppose it would be, and it appeared to me to capsize. I knew the lifeboat had been launched.

I ran home as fast as I could and told my mother and father and they said, "don't be silly the lifeboat can't capsize." Well, naturally they thought at the time it was a self-righting boat and it couldn't capsize. But anyhow, I emphasized the fact that there was a boat of some sort there and it had capsized, and she immediately got on the telephone to the coastguard station and informed them. Well, the rest the coastguards know.

32. JOHN SHARP:

Cecil's mother tried her best.

33. MRS MARCHANT:

It was very tough this morning and we went out on to the sands to see what we could see after Cecil had said that the boat had gone down, which I thought couldn't possibly go down. I didn't think a life-boat could go down, but we went out to see what we could do, down through the bungalow opening, to see if any of them washed in there, and then we were able to take them inside but no one came. Then a fisherman came along and said the boat wouldn't come in there. It would come down nearer to Broomhill, where the crevice wall came in and sure enough it did. And then we went along, Mrs. Mills and I, with the car to see what we could do; but when we got there, of course everybody was dead, so we couldn't do anything.

34. JOHN SHARP:

Mrs. Mills then living at Camber also remembers.

35. MRS. MILLS:

It was on my daughter's second birthday and my husband was lying ill in bed at the time, and I heard the maroon go, calling the lifeboat out and I went to the top of the dunes to see what was happening. I saw the lifeboat one moment and it was gone the next, so I ran back to the bungalow and made up all my beds, all the available beds, which were about four or five I suppose, and put bottles in then in the hope that I might have been of some service. but alas, it was too late, everybody died in the lifeboat.

36. JOHN SHARP:

Meanwhile back in Rye Harbour Mrs. Newton and her husband learned the truth.

37. MRS. NEWTON:

Later in the morning, I should think it was between half past ten and a quarter to eleven, my husband and I were looking through one of the upper windows of the Vicarage to see if we could see the boat return.   And we saw her return, and when she was some distance from the Harbour we suddenly saw the mast go over, and the Vicar said, "She's capsized". Then we saw the man from the beach, he was running up, he vaulted the low Vicarage wall, but we were down to meet him, and he said "Oh Sir, she's capsized".

38. JOHN SHARP:

Then the coastguards fired a maroon which the people in the village thought was a signal for the launchers to bring the boat in. But the Vicar had to go out and tell them that the boat had capsized.

39. MRS. NEWTON:

And I think I shall never, as long as I live, forget the Vicar kneeling on the beach and the women of the village kneeling with him, and the rain coming down like knitting needles, and they were praying. Well, of course, the bodies then were eventually bought back to the Harbour and put in the Fishermen's Room. All the coffins of course were alike and just the words 'Died Gallantly' put on - but I'll never never never forget the bravery of those women - they should go down in history. And well, then we had to arrange the funeral. Of course money began to pour in - vast sums came to the Vicarage and we felt we couldn't handle it and it was put in the hands of an actuary, which was a very wise thing.

40. JOHN SHARP:

The Mayor of Rye immediately launched an appeal, the response to which was enormous and world-wide. One letter from Australia was delivered to the Vicarage addressed simply, Rev. Harry Newton, B.A., England. Mrs. Reg Cooke was overseas at the time.

41. MRS COOKE:

At the time of the disaster I was in New York City, and it was a terrible shock to all the English people there: there's a large colony, of people who belong to a society known as the 'Daughters of the British Empire', and they at once set to work to raise money for the funds, by giving dances and collecting money among the people in the Society.

42. JOHN SHARP:

You heard Mrs. Newton say this fund was handled on the actuarial basis, but the Vicar's thanks were not quite so mathematical.

43. MRS NEWTON.

We got helpers in the Vicarage to help us reply to the letters, and the Vicar refused to have typewritten letters; he said every letter must be written by hand to thank these people; even little children who had sent sixpence.

44. JOHN SHARP:

Mr. William Band was father of one such child.

45. WILLIAM BAND:

I am now a resident of Rye Harbour but at the time of the disaster I lived in London. The first I heard of it was over the radio and I remember my daughter crying her eyes out. The following day she collected at her school eleven and tenpence which was forwarded to Rye.

46. JOHN SHARP:

The funeral was the biggest ever known in those parts and was attended by very many people from every possible walk of life. Needless to say, lifeboatmen and fishermen came from all over.

47. MRS NEWTON:

The day of the funeral came and really I never never would have thought that anything of the sort could have possibly happened. Now, early in the morning the crowds began to come. We had the graves all covered over with boarding because we couldn't get in the Church; there were over a thousand wreaths. It is only a little Church, and they were on the altar and the chancel, in the pulpit, down the aisles and in every pew and right at the back of the Church, and the public couldn't have got in at all; there wasn't room, so with the Churchyard being boarded over, the funeral was held round the big open grave. And that was a most remarkable time - you could have heard a pin drop, there wasn't a sound.

48. JOHN SHARP:

Frank Saunders was a bearer.

49. FRANK SAUNDERS:

Well, on the day of the funeral - my brothers and myself were to be bearers to one of my cousins - four of us, and I had two or three trips, or three or four trips to do , I'm not quite sure, but I had to go to Rye to fetch relatives and friends to be here for the actual funeral, and I know the last trip I made I only managed to get to just the Rye Harbour side of the Chemical Works and it was just chaos. I couldn't get any further at all. I had to pull the car off the road and finish by running the last three quarters of a mile to be there in time to take part in the funeral procession.

50. JACK SAUNDERS:

I lost three cousins and we attended the funeral and me and my three brothers carried one of our cousins at the funeral. I believe to be correct there was 120 pall bearers which was made of the inhabitants of the village and made up with the British Legion. It was a very big day here - I've never seen so many people in my life, not in this place.

51. JOHN SHARP:

Since 'The Mary Stanford' was lost, there has been no lifeboat at Rye Harbour. The empty lifeboat house still stands on the beach. Mrs. Ethel Caister, in a very few words, weighs up the effects of the catastrophe.

52. MRS. CAISTER:

I lost my brother in the lifeboat and also a cousin. But of course some people were much harder hit than us; but to me it seemed such a dreadful thing, because we lost all the youth of our village.

53. JOHN SHARP:

Here is Mrs. Head, widow of Albert Head the cox'n. That day she lost her husband and two of her sons. Other families were equally bereaved, but because her husband was the cox'n and a fine seaman, let her words tell what happened in her home that morning.

54. MRS. HEAD:

Well, we was in bed you see, I forget what time it was in the morning, it was early in the morning, but anyway, we were in bed, it was a very rough night, and it was blowing very hard and raining;

and presently I heard the lifeboat gun fire and my son Jack in the next bedroom. He jumped out of bed, dressed, and came downstairs and he was out of the door before his father and his other brother could get going. And I called out to Jim, my other boy, to wait for his father because it was so dark and rough, and he did wait for him, and then his father came back upstairs to say so-long to me, and I asked if he would be all right, and he said "yes, don't worry". He said, "we shall be all right". And that's how they went. That's just how they went away from the home.

I wondered how they got up to the boathouse, being such a dark rough night. I couldn't think how they could get, find a way up there. I always have wondered about that. I've never been able to go up to the Lifeboat House - I've often wanted to but never got there. I've never been able to get my heart high enough to go up and go over that path where they went.

55. JOHN SHARP:

In this programme you have heard the voices of relatives and those connected with the loss of 'The Mary Stanford'. The crew of that lifeboat had worked together, laughed together, and they died together. They are buried together: on their Memorial in the Churchyard of Rye Harbour are carved the words 'We have done that which was our duty to do'.

56. ANNOUNCER:

That was the story of the Rye Harbour Lifeboat Disaster. It was compiled and narrated by John Sharp, and was produced by Anthony Thwaite.

The 'Mary Stanford' hauled onto dry land after the disaster

This Memorial was erected on November 17th, 1931
to the memory of the crew of the
'Mary Stanford'
which capsized with the loss of all
17 lifeboatmen
on
November 15th, 1928

The Seventeen from Rye Harbour
15th November 1928 in the English Channel

A storm, far off in the Atlantic, grew
Until a full force hurricane it blew.
Along the English Channel warnings went
Of tempest and disaster imminent.

On board, ashore, then every radio station
Continuously sent out information.
All warned "Try to avoid with might and main
The dangerous centre of this Hurricane."

On board, ashore, his watch each look-out kept.
Destroying, raging, on the tempest swept.
Oh! would not many a ship and man go down
And in such mountainous water surely drown?

Now, from the English Channel, in distress,
Six ships have sent out radio S.O.S.
"Our ship is dashed to pieces by the wave."
"We're taking to the boats, Oh save us, save."

In Cherbourg, Le Havre, Dover, Isle of Wight
The life-boats stand ready to enter the fight.
All Volunteers to save in time of need,
And death would come to many in the deed.

"Hermes", the salvage tug, sent out to all
The radio S.O.S of "Pommern's" call
"We're making speed to her and if we can
We'll save from off the damaged ship each man."

Soon after midnight, ere the break of day,
A serious collision took place in Rye Bay,
One ship was holed - a coaster without light,
Her lanterns were out, she was not seen by night.

The rudder broke, the ship she sprang a leak.
Despairing, shouting, seventeen stood on deck.
They saw they drifted towards the thundering coast,
Expecting men and ship would both be lost.

Rye Harbour of the desperate call took note
And seventeen fishermen stood by the boat.
To rescue, not for praise or gain, each one
Came freely forward - father, brother, son.

They went out to rescue, all they had they gave.
Without a thought of fare, they went to save.
For often they had launched their boat before
To bring their fellow seamen to shore.

Each Harbour house was empty. The old men
And children stared across the water, then
Fearful wives and mothers could but cry
"Lord God protect us from this agony."

The boat now faced the fury of the tide
"Oh God, through surf and breaker be their guide."
Wife, mother, child thus prayed upon the shore.
But what had happened? They were seen no more.

The seventeen thought only of the call.
As made of steel and iron, against a wall
Of towering breakers, raging surf, the crew
Still held their own until they battled through.

The first to spot them was a wife, whose prayer
Was "Lord, have mercy, hear me, for out there
I have a husband and three sons aboard.
I pray You, spare their lives tonight, good Lord."

A widow woman stood there at her side,
Beseeching, praying, weeping as she cried
"Lord God, protect all of our men afloat,
I have three sons among them on this boat."

Hoping and praying, women, children, men,
Stood staring out across the water.
Then the sinking sailors saw the lifeboat too,
"They come at last" cried each to each the crew.

The seventeen lifeboat men were not afraid.
Their duty was to rescue and to aid,
Should they succeed in saving these, their name
Their gallant deed would be unknown to fame.

Now from the shore there rose a dreadful wail.
Each one had seen a thing that none dare tell -
The boat upturned, adrift and tempest tossed.
Foreboding gripped them - were the rescuers lost?

Men rushed into the raging waters then.
"Hold out! We're coming - We are with you men."
The women shrieked "Come back. Come back to shore.
They are all gone, you can do no more."

Just then the ship of those they went to save -
The other seventeen - sank in the wave.
They sent up rockets, glowing in the sky,
"Our ship is gone and we are like to die."

And they at last were saved from their distress
By "Smyrna", who first sent out the S.O.S.
From fear and tempest rescued safe and sound.
But all the Harbour seventeen were drowned.

Rye Harbour mourned the seventeen loved men,
Drowned on the fifteenth of November then.
To-day on stone, beside the church, their deed,
Their fate is written for the world to read.

By Captain B. Poppen (April 1977)

Notes :

The 'Pommern' (Pomerania) was a German full rigged ship with 60 to 80 cadets in training on board.

'Smyrna' was a freighter of the North German Lloyd. Captain Poppen, who wrote the poem, was a sailor on board at the time of the disaster.

Mrs Jacobs of Rye translated the poem from German and Mrs Goldie of Winchelsea rhymed it.

LETTER FROM POPPEN

Captain Bernhard Poppen,
Kanalstrasse 62,
2951 Stiekolkamperfehn,
West Germany.
23rd April 1977

Dear Mr Carpenter,

At your request I will gladly tell you what I remember about the tragedy of the Rye Harbour lifeboat on 15th November 1928, but as my knowledge of the English language does not permit me to write this report in English, I am writing it in German to Mrs Margaret Jacobs in Rye. She too has written me such a friendly letter that I am sure she will be so kind as to translate it into English and send it on to you. Here is the story as I remember it.

I came on board the Steamship 'Smyrna' in Bremen, as a sailor, on 10th November 1928, one week before my twentieth birthday. This ship was in regular service between the Canary Islands and Bremen/Hamburg and had a speed of about 12 knots.

We sailed from Antwerp on the afternoon of the 14th November. The wind was from the West, strong to storm force; real autumn weather. Towards midnight we passed Dover, the wind increased, at times heavy squalls. The sea was very rough and our ship pitched and rolled to such an extent that we had to reduce speed. In the hurricane like squalls huge masses of water poured over the forepart of the ship. The Captain, the second officer, the look-out man, the helmsman and a reserve, kept watch on the bridge. In the early hours of the night several S.O.S. radio signals were received - all calls for help from ships in the English Channel.

The German training ship 'Pommern' (Pomerania) was among those in distress. Her S.O.S. signal was received by our ship, but the distance was too great for us to render assistance. I wrote about the fate of the 'Pommern' in a newspaper article and, as I assume that you too may be interested in view of the connection with the Rye tragedy, I append you an account.

THE LOSS OF THE TRAINING SHIP 'POMMERN'

One of the last (sail) German training ships still in existence has become a victim of the November storms. The sail training ship 'Pommern' of the German Training Ship's Company was on voyage from the Canary Islands to Plymouth. Shortly before reaching her destination, about 80 sea miles south of Lands End, she sank when, in a severe squall, all her masts went overboard. All 84 of her crew, which included the officers who were training and the young men who wished to become seamen, were rescued by the Hamburg salvage tug 'Heros'. Four British ships also hurried to the rescue. One of them, the 'Lancastria', lowered a life-boat but, owing to the rough seas, it was not possible to reach the 'Pommern' and the boat had to turn back. With the greatest difficulty the crew were got back on board, but the boat itself was smashed by the sea.

I will now continue my story:

Our 'Smyrna' could only proceed very slowly. The furious squalls whipped up the mountainous waves and the ship was rolled and pitched about like a ball. At about 3.30 in the morning, when approaching Beachy Head, a shuddering shock ran through the whole ship. We had rammed the 'Alice' which was showing no stern light. We knew that something terrible had happened, but we could see nothing. Our Captain immediately ordered the engines astern. This brought our ship into a very dangerous situation.

After waiting many anxious moments we saw light signals from the 'Alice'. She reported that her stern was badly damaged, her rudder and engines had dropped off and the ship was therefore unmanoeuverable. There was already a lot of water in the engine-room, the wind and the sea would soon drive the ship ashore. Because of the heavy surf the ship would have to be abandoned before this happened.

We now stood by the 'Alice' as close as was possible. Both ships, driven by wind and storm, were often in great danger. It was impossible to get a line across. Our Captain called for volunteers to man our lifeboat. At first light the crew of the 'Alice' were to be taken off. This was too risky to attempt in darkness. Our lifeboat hung in the davits ready for lowering. We had also lowered ropes, life buoys, ladders etc. on the leeside and had taken all the necessary measures so that, if possible, no lives should be lost.

Between 5 and 6 o'clock the 'Alice' suddenly flashed a light signal that the crew had taken to the boats. It took a little time before we could see them. With great difficulty our Captain succeeded in manoeuvering his ship near to the boat. The crew of the 'Smyrna' were spaced along the lee side of the ship near to the boat. At every opportunity life lines were thrown across to the tossing boat of the 'Alice' to which the men tied themselves to and we pulled them up to our ship. Some of the bravest managed to seize the right moment to jump over to our ship.

However, the situation became more and more dangerous. There were still three men in the boat who seemed unable to make up their minds to jump either in to death or into life. Then a huge wave crushed the tiny boat against our side. My comrade and I each managed to grab hold of a man, the third leaped out of the boat and was luckily able to seize hold of one of the ladders which was floating out on a line, and so was dragged on board by our men. They were all saved and the Captain immediately broadcast the message.

The shipwrecked men were to be put ashore a few hours later at Dover. But this could not be done because, owing to the storm, it was not possible to put in to Dover. So we set course for Antwerp. The orders were changed several times, so that we did not arrive there until 20th November, my twentieth birthday, and there we put the shipwrecked men ashore.

Unfortunately I can no longer remember for certain whether there were 14 or 17 men; for I have both numbers in mind. But I do know for sure that there was a woman (the cook) among them, for my companion and I pulled her out of the water.

The 'Alice' was a kind of coaster or collier, an old ship, with (as far as I know) a cargo of bricks. As her rudder and engines had fallen out and the engine room had a large leak, the ship could not remain afloat and had to be abandoned.

The cause of the disaster was that the stern lanterns on the 'Alice' were not lit. However, it is possible that the heavy weather and the waves breaking over the ship had put them out.

This, my dear Mr Carpenter, is what I remember. In the years 1929/30 I heard and read a number of times about the tragic death of the Rye Harbour life boat crew, and I have always been so deeply stirred and moved by this tragedy, in which I too played a part at sea, that, in my old age, I have described the whole incident, as far as I can remember it, in a poem "The Seventeen from Rye Harbour".

I hope I have been of some service to you, and remain, with friendly greetings.

Yours faithfully, (signed) B. Poppen.

Rye Harbour Lifeboat Station

LIVES RESCUED BY THE LIFE BOATS MANNED
BY THE INTREPID MEN OF THE RYE HARBOUR LIFEBOAT

First Life Boat

			People Rescued
1852	Aug. 15th	`Brig 'AVON' of London	3

Second Life Boat

1862	Dec 10th	American ship 'JAMES BROWN'		18
1867	Jan 3rd	Barque 'MARIE AMELIE' of Quintes		14
		Assisted to save vessel	Total	32

Third Life Boat: "THE STORM SPRITE"

1867	Oct 22nd	Ship 'MICHIELS LOOS' of Antwerp		
		Remained by vessel		
1869	Feb 14th	Brig 'PEARL' of Shoreham		8
1871	Jan 16th	Brig 'ELIZABETH & CICELY' of Guernsey		8
1371	Dec 18th	Barge 'ROBINA' of North Shields		8
1874	Feb 25th	Schooner 'HELENE' of Crutz		4
1876	Jan 21st	Brig 'FRED THOMSON' of Dundee		
		Remained by vessel		
1877	Dec 22nd	Schooner 'VIER BRODERS' of Groningen		4
1878	Jun 28th	Schooner 'FEARLESS' of Guernsey		6
			Total	38

Fourth Life Boat: "THE FRANCES HARRIS"

		Placed on this station 21st Feb 1883		
1884	Jan 23rd	Brig 'SILKSWORTH' of Blyth		7
1890	Dec 4th	Steam tug No. 15 of Plymouth		6
		Assisted to save the vessel		
1891	Dec 28th	Barque 'WARWICKSHIRE' of London		18
			Total	31
1896	Dec 5th	'S.S. MENZALEH' of London		
		Rendered assistance		

Fifth Life Boat: "THE JOHN WILLIAMS DUDLEY"

		Placed on this station 12th Oct 1900		
1900	Oct 25th	German ship 'HELICON'		
		Rendered assistance		

1901	Jan 19th	Smack 'JEUNE ARTHUR' of Cherburg		4
1902	Feb 23rd	Ketch 'PILOT' of Plymouth		
		saved vessel		4
1904	Feb 20-25th	'S.S. LAKE MICHIGAN' of Liverpool		
		Stood by vessel		
1904	May 2nd	Ship 'DERWENT' of London		
		Stood by vessel		
1905	Jun 22nd	'S.S. CLARA' of London		
		Stood by vessel		
1907	Jan 22nd	Ketch 'LORD TENNYSON' of London		3
1907	Mar 18th	'S.S. SWAN of Sunderland		
		Stood by Vessel		
1909	Dec 22nd	'S.S. SALATIS' of Hamburg		
		Rendered assistance and boat		
		of tug 'OCEANA' of London		3
			Total	14
1910	Mar 9th	Steam trawler 'MARGARET' of Rye		
		Stood by vessel		
1912	Dec 26th	'S.S. BEDEBURN' of Newcastle		
	27th	Assisted to save vessel		
1916	Apr 17th	'S.S. KIRNWOOD' of Middlesbrough		
		Rendered assistance		

Sixth Life Boat: "THE MARY STANFORD"

1920	May 28th	'S.S. THURA FREDRIKKE' of Poisground		
		Stood by vessel		
1921	Mar 29th	Barge 'LADY ELLEN' of Woodbridge		2
1923	Dec 13th	An aeroplane		2
		Salvaged aeroplane	Total	8

Total lives saved in all 128

The 'Mary Stanford' was capsized with the loss of the whole of her crew of seventeen, on the 15th November 1928, after she had been launched to the help of the 'S.S. Alice' of Riga, in a whole South West gale with a very heavy sea.

The Station was temporarily closed following the disaster and permanently closed in July 1929.

THE BOAT

In May 1914 the Royal National Lifeboat Institution offered a new lifeboat to the Rye Harbour Station and 3 people were invited, (coxswain and two crew members), to visit 3 other lifeboat stations to see the different types of boat working under the same conditions as those at Rye Harbour.

They chose a Liverpool type class surf boat, specially constructed for the type of flat coastline to be found in the Rye area. These boats were large, stable and were able to go well out to sea, although not able to self right. Self-righting boats were heavier, drew more water and would have been difficult to launch from Rye Harbour Station. Not all locals agreed with this choice, but it was the local crew who had the final say.

The 'Mary Stanford' was built in 1916 by S.E. Saunders Ltd. at East Cowes, on the Isle of Wight, and was tested there for stability and draught, on April 13th 1916. She was a pulling and sailing boat, propelled by oars and a close-reefed mainsail. She was 38ft long by 10ft 9in wide, and her weight complete was 4 tons 12¼ cwts.

The new lifeboat was sailed from East Cowes to Rye Harbour by the crew and was placed on service at the Station on October 19th 1916. On November 25th of that year, a test exercise was carried out at Rye under bad weather conditions, which severely tested the boat's capabilities. She handled excellently and the crew had complete faith in the 'Mary Stanford'.

Whilst at Rye Harbour, she was launched on 63 occasions - 47 times for practice and 16 times for actual rescue.

THE CREW

The crew of the Rye Harbour lifeboat were all taken from village volunteers. Many of them were fisherman so, of course, they were experienced seamen.

They had all grown up together so they were friends and they worked with each other in the small, inter-related community.

The crew of the 'Mary Stanford' on the day of November 15th 1928 was:

	Age
Herbert Head, coxswain	47
Joseph Stonham, second coxswain	43
Henry Cutting, bowman,	39
Albert Ernest Smith	44
Walter Igglesden	38
Charles Frederick David Pope	28
Roberts Redvers Cutting	28
William Thomas Albert Clark	27
Albert Ernest Cutting	26
Arthur William Downey	25
Leslie George Clark	24
Robert Henry Pope	23
Charles Southerden	22
Lewis Alexander Pope	21
James Alfred Head	19
John Stanley Read	17

THE 'MARY STANFORD' LIFEBOAT

(From the Rye Gazette, published by Mary Owen in 1984)

Two years ago, in its report on the 1982 lifeboat memorial service, the GAZETTE asked "who was Mary Stanford?". We had some feedback, though not much; but it included a puzzling reference to another 'Mary Stanford' lifeboat at Ballycotton in Eire.

Sheila Draffin, of West Street, has a sister living near Ballycotton, as well as friends in the fishing community there, and she offered to investigate on behalf of the GAZETTE. We also made enquiries from the RNLI, and are most grateful to Miss Draffin and to Mrs. Griffiths at Poole for their help with this account.

There were, it seems, three 'Mary Stanford' lifeboats.

Mr. John Frederick Stanford of Regent's Park died in 1880 or 1881, leaving money to the RNLI to endow a lifeboat to be named after his Mother. This was stationed at Rye "to take place of the former boat stationed near Camber Coastguard Station not far from the entrance of the Harbour". The first 'Mary Stanford' was 34 foot long and rowed ten oars double-banked, says 'The Lifeboat' reporting the launching ceremony on 8th September 1881. "After proceeding through the Town of Rye, the boat was taken to the Strand, where a large concourse had assembled, numbering some four or five thousand people. Addresses were delivered by the Mayor of Rye (Mr. Henry Burra), General Kerr (Mr. Stanford's cousin and executor), Mr. F. A. Inderwick MP, and the District Inspector of Life-Boats... the Rev. T. D. Gladstone offered up a prayer for the success of the boat.... Mrs. Kerr performed the naming ceremony."

She went out 11 times in the next ten years, saving 35 lives, and was replaced in due course by 'Edward and Lucile' (launched only twice before the station was closed in 1901.)

It seems likely that the reason for the Camber Station's closure was the arrival in 1900 at what was then called the Winchelsea Station of a much larger boat - costing £831 as against under £400 - the 'John William Dudley'. Her replacement we all know about; the second 'Mary Stanford'. She came to Rye in 1916, having cost just over £2000 to build; she was launched 16 times, saved 10 lives, and capsized with the loss of all 17 crew members, on 15 November 1928.

After this disaster, the Stanford family wished to give the RNLI a replacement boat. In 1929 Ballycotton, a small fishing port on the south coast of Ireland was due for a new boat (its sixth), and RNLI officials went over to talk to the crew. Miss Draffin's friend, whose late husband had been a member of the Ballycotton crew for very many years, recalls that the RNLI representatives spoke to each crew member individually to ask if he minded having a boat with the same name as the one which had only recently brought tragedy to Rye Harbour. Without exception all the crewmen agreed that the name should be carried on. It would, they said, be a tribute to the Rye Harbour boat and its crew, who had been defeated only by the elements.

So, in 1930 at Ballycotton, the third 'Mary Stanford' went into service. She cost well over £9000, and had a most satisfactory career over the next thirty years. She was launched 83 times, saved 101 lives, and in 1936 made a particularly dramatic rescue of eight men from the Daunt Rock lightship. In 1959 she was replaced by the present Ballycotton boat, the 'Ethel Mary'; 'Mary Stanford' became a standby boat, and was later sold for use as a pilot boat at Shannon.

It is hardly surprising that after more than a hundred years the RNLI has no details of the original Stanford legacy. But it is perfectly reasonable to assume that if John Stanford died in 1880, his mother could have been born in the late 1770's. It does seem odd that after possibly 200 years we still remember the name of this lady, but nothing else about her.

❖ ❖ ❖

Camber Castle

78

CHAPTER 8

AN INTERVIEW WITH MR TED CAISTER

I was about 9 years of age when evacuated to Marston Martaine which is about nine miles from the town of Bedford. Also evacuated to the same village were four of my brothers and my sister. My eldest brother was old enough for, initially, the Home Guard and later the Army.

Other children from Rye Harbour spent various times there as well. Although most of my family were billeted in this village, I seldom saw any of them outside school or Church. My misfortune was to be billeted with two different families, both of whom were of strong religious persuasion and seemed to object to me wanting to mix with my family and friends socially, or for sport and working in the fields at harvest time. This was decidedly the most unhappy time of my life and that eighteen months still makes me shudder when recalled.

Upon my return to Rye Harbour in early 1943, it was to find that various houses, the school, the Vicarage and one of the two public houses had been taken over as accommodation for the Army. This was much enjoyed by the now returned children of the village and, of course, we spent a lot of time in the company of the soldiers. One amusing incident during this period was when a few children managed to start up a Brenn gun carrier [a small tank like vehicle] and drive it straight through the doors of its garage, needless to say, by the time the soldiers arrived on the scene, the vehicle was deserted.

Many friendships were formed with the soldiers during their stay and it was with great sadness that the village learned that almost the entire Company was wiped out when the Allied Forces invaded France to commence the freeing of Occupied Europe.

During the build up to the invasion, the Royal Navy also came to Rye Harbour, just prior to what we learned was to be known as 'D-Day'. The river was stem to stern with tank landing craft and personnel carrying ships. One day a ship of this type was entering the Harbour on a swiftly flowing tide and the crew were standing to attention as a salute to a high ranking officer standing on the jetty returning the salute. The ship just clipped the jetty, sending the crew tumbling into the hold one after the other. This was viewed with much amusement by quite a crowd of villagers standing on the river bank. Fortunately none of the sailors were seriously hurt.

During this time movement around the village was very restricted and then allowed only on the production of the correct identity card. The Army, obviously better informed than the villagers, were beginning to show a few nerves and on at least one occasion fired at our own aircraft.

Once the Army and Navy had left, then fishing and farming became the main topics of conversation.

A few days of excitement were created about this time by a large American bomber crash-landing on the sand of the foreshore. It was a Boeing Flying Father and it had limped back over the Channel, where it had been damaged by gunfire. It did a couple of circles before doing a perfect 'pancake' landing on the sand without injury to any of the crew.

The most frightening period for the villagers in Rye Harbour was when the Germans introduced the 'DOODLE BUG'. This was a jet propelled pilotless aircraft full of high explosives. The Doodle Bug was launched via a ramp from the coast of France with enough fuel to reach London. Quite frequently, due to mechanical failure, local gunfire or interception by Allied planes, they crashed in or around the village

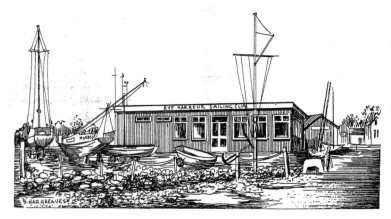

Rye Harbour Sailing Club

CHAPTER 9

AN INTERVIEW WITH MRS PAT GAWN (née CAISTER)
Given to Emma Caister

I was 16 years old when World War II broke out. At the time I was working in my first job in the office at the Chemical Works, but I left and worked for Winter's Dairy in Cinque Ports St., delivering milk in the town. I used to get up at 5 am every morning and get to work by 6 am. In the winter, when there was snow on the ground, I used to walk, but any other time, I used to cycle with my friend Molly Southerden. She went on up to Watlands Farm Udimore, to milk the cows. Each side of our village (Camber and Winchelsea Beach) were evacuated, which left us rather on our own.

We were each issued with identity cards with our picture on them, and those of us who had to cross over the bridge at the top of the road, had to report to the sentry who was on guard there in a sentry box. When we had done our day's work, the same thing happened on our way home. As the War progressed, I wanted to do something else. So I went to Slough in Buckinghamshire to learn to work on aircraft. I trained to be a fitter working in 'Spitfires'.

I had a head start when I was given the job of packing parachutes, as my grandfather, Jim Downey, had taught me how to splice rope. I also had an advantage when I used to fit compasses, which were right up in the nose of the plane. I was small and I could get up there easier than most. When I passed out as a fitter, I went to Reading Aerodrome in Berkshire to work on 'Spitfires' which had been damaged in battle, and indeed, any other aircraft also.

One day a Lancaster Bomber made an emergency landing, and among the crew who walked out of the hangar was my 6ft.3in. tall cousin, Norman Caister! Neither of us could believe the coincidence! His parents kept the 'William the Conqueror' at that time.

I got married in 1944 at Rye Harbour Church and some relations, who were coming from Shoreham for the wedding, all had to go to Rye Police Station first, to get passes to be allowed by the Sentry at the top of Rye Harbour Road to come to the Harbour. They all had to leave the village before dark too!

My family used to get very worried about me and my "war work", as it was called, but in fact, there was a great feeling of comradeship. We shared a shelter in Tram Road under the house belonging to Mr Alec Coleman.

I don't think Rye Harbour has changed a great deal, people are still friendly and a good many of them are related. No one in trouble has to look far for help. I think this applies to most small villages. There is still not a lot of work down here, most people have to leave the village for employment. The 'Mary Stanford Green' is a very well laid out estate and fits in with the village.

RYE HARBOUR IN WORLD WAR II

Rye Harbour received 61 H.E. bombs; 380 incendiaries; and 4 attacks by machine gun and cannon fire. This resulted in 4 persons being killed and 9 injured.

CHAPTER 10

'RESOLUTE' AT DUNKIRK
by MR A.W. JOSELYNE

The 'Resolute', bought by Mr Alan 'Dusty' Miller in 1969, is moored on Admiralty Wharf, Rye Harbour. This Chapter, written by Mr Joselyne, records his brother Vincent's recollections of his voyage in her, in 1940. The 'Resolute' was sailed across to Dunkirk again in 1990, for the 50th Anniversary of the Evacuation, and has a brass plaque recording this voyage. Mr Joselyne himself went to the Dunkirk beaches and has written of the voyages on the 'Sun III' and 'Shannon'.

"My brother Vincent and I got separated an signing on at the Thames Control Centre, Southend. He made his way to the Pier Head alone. He revealed, later, to my amazement, that he too had at first been assigned to 'Renown' - only to be told that her crew was complete. I could hardly believe that all of us had, by the mercy of Providence, been saved from the fate that overtook this little boat, and her gallant crew.

Having left 'Renown', my brother came to 'Resolute', moored close by, and, at his suggestion, was taken on to augment her crew of two. At 10.30, the tiny fleet of Leigh cockle boats - 'Renown', 'Reliance', 'Resolute', 'Defender', 'Endeavour', and 'Letitia' - set off under the command of a Naval Officer on their way to the beaches of Dunkirk, where they arrived around seven o'clock the same day, In the middle of a bombing raid. All Hell was, it seemed, let loose. The pom poms and machine guns from the destroyers and other craft mingled with the crash of bombs, and the scream of enemy dive bombers struck terror into, and wreaked mass murder among the troops lined up in formation on the shore. Wreckage and carnage and the smell of burning oil was everywhere.

In the middle of all this, the little fleet was ordered to go ashore, pick up as many troops as possible and return to a larger vessel, identified by a green light, to unload. When given this order by their Naval Commander, a man obviously not versed in the knowledge of fishermen used to tidal shallow water, the crews refused to obey, because they all knew the result would have been fatal. The

83

tide was falling rapidly and immediately their boats grounded, soldiers would clamber aboard, fill them to capacity and set them hard and fast on the bottom. The ebbing tide would leave them high and dry and in an equal, if not worse, danger than they already were. So it was agreed that they would go alongside a long concrete arm, known as the 'mole', in deeper water. 'Resolute', with her companions, proceeded to the mole and, in an orderly manner, in the teeth of the fury going on all around, British soldiers were embarked to fill the little vessels to capacity,

And there arose a curious question. My brother, at this point, mentioned that these were all officers. When I queried this, he insisted that they were not, as he said, ordinary soldiers. I later found out that these officers were, in fact, engaged in office and routine jobs and had not been in combat!

'Resolute' cast off fully loaded, (my brother estimates 50 or 60 men), with dusk and mist closing in and made her way out into deeper water looking for the promised green light. Owing, he thinks, to the heavy air attacks taking place, the waiting ships had up anchored and disappeared. After cruising around searching for some considerable time, an officer asked him what he thought he was doing, to which he replied he had no more idea than his passenger. The orders were to find a green light - which wasn't there - and if the officer could show him where it was, he would do his best to satisfy him. The officer said that as far as he could see, they'd be just as well off ashore as paddling around out there and suggested they go back again. He was obviously a man who preferred to be on dry land, however uncomfortable that dry land was at that moment. Vincent replied that under no circumstances was he going back, but very shortly afterwards the situation was resolved for them by a dark shape looming up out of the darkness, which turned out to be a large steam drifter. Hailing the skipper on the bridge, 'Resolute's' crew were delighted to hear an English voice.

The skipper of the drifter took on 'Resolute's' passengers and my brother and his companions learned that the ship intended to return to Ramsgate. Not knowing what to do, they asked whether they could hitch up to the drifter and go back with her, and this was agreed. Shortly afterwards, others of the little fleet appeared and, discharging their passengers aboard the drifter, tied up with the 'Resolute'.

At this point, the Naval Officer in command turned up in another cockle boat and immediately ordered any of them that were still serviceable to return and collect more troops. By now it was nearly midnight and things were much quieter, so it was decided to go right into the harbour and lay up on a pier.

A destroyer lay sunk across the entrance; oil barrels and debris of all descriptions floated on the oily waters. As they entered the harbour, distinguished by their phosphorescent wakes, they could see on one side, one of the 'Eagle' steamers as she lay sinking, a bomb having scored a direct hit down her funnel. The wreckage of vehicles showed here and there above the water. Making their way slowly through this mess, they drew alongside the pier and were soon again filled to overflowing with soldiers. They were followed by the 'Letitia', also fully loaded and, passing a towline between them to keep together, carefully threaded their way out of the harbour into the darkness beyond.

They found no boats awaiting them. So, keeping going, although crammed with their human cargo, they found their way back across the Channel and eventually fetched Ramsgate, where they landed the troops they had saved around seven o'clock that morning. Immediately after unloading, they all set off for home, dropping anchor in the Bay about four thirty in the afternoon. From all accounts they celebrated their return in the usual manner at the Half Way House in Southend the following day.

Having listened to my brother's story, I have endeavoured to relate it as accurately as possible. Little incidents such as the time when he asked a soldier for a drink of water from his water bottle and found he was drinking neat brandy, were incidental. Also the story of how, when the soldiers were coming aboard, an officer gave up his place and pushing a soldier forward said "His wife is expecting a baby next week. Take him." And the young soldier who threw himself off the pier and drowned, because there was no room to take him. These little human stories, and many like them, went unrecorded in the light of the major and historic events taking place all around them, and in most cases got lost in the official history of this event.

There is one curious discrepancy.   In this story, my brother seems very sure that the 'Resolute, and the 'Letitia' entered and left the harbour at Dunkirk together, attached by a tow line. That they unloaded at Ramsgate together and arrived, still together, at Leigh with no other of their fleet.   But from all other accounts, it would seem that when the 'Renown' was blown up by a floating mine and all her crew were lost, she was being towed by the 'Letitia' because her engine had broken down, and so she was lost too.   Obviously both stories cannot be true, but Vincent seems very sure of his version.

I asked his reactions and feelings during the time of his ordeal and his answer was that it was so packed with action and effort, he had no time to think of what might happen, only what was happening all around them at that particular moment.   We, on the other hand, saw little violent action, just the constant anticipation of what might or could happen and the complete helplessness of anything we could do, either to protect ourselves or fight back.   Even our two days stay at anchor within sight of Ramsgate, the ever present danger of air or sea attack and even invasion, was constantly and ever present, as was the prospect of returning to Calais.   These were two completely different aspects of the same operation, and which was the more traumatic I am still not sure.   To complete this story on a happy note, my wife's three brothers, Frederick, John and Henry Harvey, all serving with B.E.F. in France, were all rescued at Dunkirk by the little ships and arrived back in England safe and well.   In retrospect, I wish I had also asked for and recorded their particular stories - unfortunately two have passed on - so their story, like so many others, will remain untold.

The new Rye Harbour Lifeboat Station

CHAPTER 11

RYE HARBOUR VISIT, MARCH 1945; MAXINE BALDRY.

The first time I visited Rye Harbour was on a bleak March day in 1945. The visiting restrictions had been lifted for "unauthorised personnel". My brother, who was a sergeant in the USA Air Force, my sister-in-law and I, caught a bus from the Castle Hotel in Hastings on a day when the rain was just holding off. The skies were grey with low cloud misting the views and a gusty East wind was blowing.

We had an early lunch for five shillings at the George Hotel, which consisted of thick brown soup tasting the way wrapping paper smells, roast lamb, boiled potatoes, well boiled cabbage, suet pudding with thick custard and indescribable coffee in front of a roaring fire.

Leaving the warmth and comfort of Rye, we walked to the Harbour and never met a soul. The main road was like a deserted village, windows taped and some boarded up. Around the Point, the tide was out and 'Zephyr' stood in the midst of coils of rolled up barbed wire looking like big bramble bushes, which were spaced all around the Harbour and the railway.

On the railway line stood empty goods waggons; there were boats tied up but no sign of a human being. There were no men in the pub and the only drinks available were Old, Mild or Bitter, Cider, or Pale Ale. No one was chatty so we drank up; I believe Fred Caister was home on leave and he and my brother had a bit of Air Force talk (not particularly friendly but not hostile either). We then had a quick game of darts, another drink and it was not only pub time, but our bus left the top of the Rye Harbour road in about 35 minutes.

Great panics to put on coats, hats, gloves, scarves and say good-byes and off we went (jogging is just the right word for it). We had a good ten minutes to spare as we waited for our chariot which was quite full. It took us back to Hastings before the evening blackout and in time for tea.

CHAPTER 12

A MEMORY OF RYE HARBOUR - 1947
Written in August 1980

The early February dusk was closing in. On the road to the shore the "Look-Out" towered some 60ft into the darkening sky, challenging one's last energies to climb it. Once up on that lofty perch there seemed no life at all in that solitary landscape, but, far below, a figure could be seen trudging down the Eastern side of the Rother to light the paraffin lamps. These steady guiding lights were the beacons for incoming boats, and many seafarers preferred them to the flashing signals which later replaced them. In the old clock tower the lights shone out as well, signifying the depth of water in the river. It could have been another time - another age, but the concrete pill-box on the foreshore bore testimony to the struggle of war-time, and the threat of invasion only a few years before.

In those days it was possible to wander at all points of the compass around Rye Harbour. One could walk up the grassy track of the old railway line towards Rye and, in the perfect quietude of those days, with myriads of oyster catchers, red shanks and dunlins, it was uninterrupted in its setting. To the East was the ferry taking people to work at Camber - push bikes as well - and a favourite outing was to ramble over the dunes returning at dusk to be ferried across the river by Johnnie Doughty and later by that other, salty character (Arthur Sellwood) affectionately known as "Sally". Perhaps a vivid, lasting glimpse of another sight soon to be over was that of the Vicar being ferried over the river on Sunday mornings.

In good weather he could be seen in his cassock striding over the golf course to take a service at the sister Church at Camber.

Behind the Martello Tower stretched the fields full of grazing sheep and, in the distance - Camber Castle. Built by Henry VIII on a spit of shingle as a coastal defence, it was a crumbling ruin - its walls thick with ivy and the old castle itself full of exciting tunnels and uneven levels to explore. The Ministry of Works cast a speculative eye on this old pile, and decided to take it under its all embracing wing and close it to the public. So it remains to this day [Now can be seen by public. Ed.].

On the shore the shrimping nets could be seen drying above the high water mark, each one recognisable so that no names were needed, and tools could be left around for days at a time without fear of losing them. Amongst the boating fraternity a free and easy relationship existed, and it was not unusual to notice the sails of one's boat out on the sea and realise that a friend had taken it for a trip.

Nostalgia is a luxury. To-day Rye Harbour is very definitely on the map. The river teams with life - and the coasters particularly - bring a taste of foreign travel to our shores. The visitors freed from the confines of their high rise flats, and suburban semi-detached houses swarm around Rye Harbour. Many never leave their cars at all, but fall asleep in the sun and fresh air behind their newspapers to awake renewed for the journey home. We continue to be amazed - and (dare I say it?) proud - that this small corner of Sussex has so much to offer.

❖ ❖ ❖

Rye Harbour Nature Reserve

CHAPTER 13

THE BURNING OF THE BARGE : BY MAXINE BALDRY

Just a roof over my head was all I wanted when we were laying up or fitting out 'Zephyr'.   Kindly folk would take me and the children into the warmth of their homes, but it was an imposition, during sudden rain sleet storms. I shall never forget their kindnesses.

Late in the 1940's or early 1950's, we bought the derelict barge belonging to Mr Weatherseed, which lay behind the present ships' chandlers.   Only the wheelhouse was intact.   Inside was a coal-wood stove on which one could cook and which heated most of the living space.   The decks were dangerous and the hull had been stripped of most fittings.   The name of the barge was 'Orient'.   She had been a cement carrier on the Medway and in the Thames.   After the Weatherseeds had bought her in 1923, she had been fitted out in Hinds Yard, Rye, with teak and satinwood fittings.   She did not sail very well as a yacht-barge; she needed more ballast to keep her steady and comfortable.   The Weatherseed family used her less and less after they bought the 'Spero' from RNLI in 1929.   The 'Orient' was lent to the harbour master for living accommodation while his house was being built on the Camber side of the river.   Afterwards she fell into disrepair and WWII saw her decline into a hulk.

However, we were very pleased to own her and used her often. One day Johnny Doughty rang up to say some child in the Harbour had been caught up by his arm, while climbing over the decks which collapsed.   Jack, being a solicitor, was very anxious about this, being uninsured for third party and things I'd never considered.   We knew the wheel house was being used in our absence, but had assumed it was more for romantic purposes than youngsters deering-do!!

Great consultations and much beer at the Conq. resulted in the giving over of the Barge for Rye Harbour's Bonfire Night.   We were not involved in the preparations, but we, like everyone else, brought fireworks.   Outside the pub someone got a workman's brazier going full blast, on which bloaters and roast jacket potatoes were cooked. A giant sing-song roared out of the pub windows, while the bloaters and spuds were passed in.   Someone made a bit of pocket money that night!

Johnny Doughty lit the fire with the help of small boys and others. He was the most upset sailor I have ever seen as the old boat went up in flames. We were all moved to see her burning from end to end, an unforgettable moment in my own life and another mark on the pages of village history. I understand she smouldered for two days until the tide finally quenched the embers.

The Watch House

CHAPTER 14

"VALENTINE'S DAY"
(written in the Church Magazine, Feb.1981)

In a little monograph about the "Lovers Seat", Fairlight published in Victorian times by an unnamed author, there is a link with Rye Harbour. As the stones which formed the lovers seat have had to be salvaged from the crumbling cliffs and replaced higher up and further back, perhaps a thought might be given to the original lovers.

The only daughter, Elizabeth, of Mr Samuel Boys of Elford, Hawkhurst, Kent, fell in love with Mr Charles Lamb, Captain, R.N. officer in the Preventive Service and Commanding Officer of the Revenue Cutter 'STAG' based at Rye Harbour.

Mr Boys did not approve of the association and sent his daughter to a farm at Fairlight, in the hope that the change of air might diminish her passion for Captain Lamb.

It would be wonderful to examine the log of 'STAG' to see how many hours patrol were spent near Fairlight, for the lovers did meet and their relationship developed, until they eloped and were married on 16th January, 1786 at St. Clement Danes, in the Strand, London.

Mr Boys never forgave his daughter and disinherited her. Captain Lamb resigned his commission. He built a house in Salehurst called 'Highman'. There, one daughter was born, who eventually married the Reverend Thomas Ferris, eldest son of Thomas Ferris, D.D., Dean of Battle. Captain Lamb never lost his love for the sea, but unfortunately he was drowned while sailing his yacht in Southampton Water in 1814. Mrs Lamb lived on to enjoy her grandchildren.

There are so many interesting lines to follow in this story. Was Captain Lamb a member of the Rye family of Lamb? Is the log of the 'Stag' available? Did the lovers, before being separated, meet at the parties, manor houses and assemblies in Rye, Icklesham, Northiam and Battle? Are there any records of these occasions? Is 'Highman' still extant? We must search out some of the answers, but if anyone has any clues, please let us know.

CHAPTER 15

RYE HARBOUR DUES

(A page taken from the Harbour Dues Book)

SMACKS

Name of Vessel	Rates per quarter	Date	Info.
Albert	9s	1898-1902	
A&LG (G. Fowle)	8s 6d	1898-1902	
Alice	10s	1898-1902	
Alice & Rebecca	10s	1898-1899	Laid-up
		1901-1902	
Annie (B. Breeds)	12s	1898-1902	
Annie (F. Tarrell)	8s	1898-1902	
Athena	6s	1898-1902	
Bee	11s 6d	1898-1899	Sold
Bessie (W. Mills)	3s 6d	1898-1899	Laid-up
Bessie (W. Southerden)	5s	1898-1899	Broken up
British Queen	12s	1898-1901	Laid up.
Choice (Farrell)	10s	1898-1902.	
Couster	12s	1898-1902	
Crusader	4s	1898-1899	Finished fishing
Daisy	11s 6d	1898-1902	
Ellen	11s 6d	1898-1902	
Fancy	12s	1898-1902	
Fanny	7s 6d	1898-1899	Laid-up
Florence	10s 6d	1898-1902	
Forget-me-not	11s 6d	1898-1902	
Freedom (Albert Barrett owner)			
	7s 6d	1898-1902	
Gipsey (J. W. Smith)			Laid up
Godild	9s 6d	1898-1900	Laid-up.
Harry Lepper	8s	1898-1902	
Louie	11s	1898-1902	
Louisa (J. W. Smith)			Laid up
Lucy	10s 6d	1898-1902	
Maid of Kent	9s 6d	1898-1899	Laid-up. Only fit to be broken up.

RENTS

(This is another page from the Harbour Master's Accounts. A small newspaper cutting was stuck to the page which helps us to understand what the rents were for.)

Name	Rate per year	Date
S. Gallop	5s	1909-1913
H. J. Gasson	80s half year	1909-1912
do.	30s do.	1909-1912
do.	10s do.	1909-1911

"Mr H. J. Gasson being desirous of surrendering his lease of the wooden hut near the Harbour Lighthouse, such surrender being accepted. We recommend that a new lease thereof be granted to Mr T. Symonds Vidler, on the same terms, viz. 10s per annum, for a period of 14 years."

"This report was adopted, the Mayor stating that when the sluice gates were worked more the sand would move out of the bed of the river. The Corporation had paid them a fair price for the hire of the dredger. They had received between 20 and 30 complaints respecting the old building near the lighthouse, it had been a very great eyesore for many years, but they had received a revenue of 10s from Mr Gasson. Mr J. Symonds Vidler was going to take it over for a period of 14 years and he would do it up and use it for an office".

A. E. Hinds	40s	1909-1913
A. Simpson	10s	1909-1913
EPNS Jones	5s	1909-1913
do.	10s	1909-1917
do.	40s	1909-1917
James Ney	25s	1909-1917
H. J. Phillips	110s	1909-1917
K.Reeve	1s	1909-1916
do.	2s	1909-1916
do.	2s	1909-1916

"The Sanitary Committee reported that they had arranged with the Rye Harbour Commissioners to determine the hiring of the scavenger's enclosure, Pollard's Wharf, on March 16th next (Report 5 Dec. 1913.) The Inspector was pressing on with the work of seeing that flushing tanks were *installed in all the houses in the Borough which required them. Alderman Jarrett, in moving the adoption of the report, said they had been asked if they could give up the lease of Pollard's Wharf earlier than the date named, but the Council would probably require to use the land when the New Bridge was closed for repairs, as they would not be able to have access to the new depot over the river."*

RYE HARBOUR : SMALL BOAT DUES.

Name of Vessel	Rate per ½ Yr.	Name	Years	
AEJ	5s	J. Jewhurst	1918-24	
Boy Charlie	5s	F. W. Tillman	1918-21	LU
Boy Jim	5s	S. Robus	1918-22	LU
Elsie	5s	Geo. Fowler	1918-24	
Emma	5s	Walt. Caister	1918-21	LU
Endeavour	5s	Bert. Downey	1918-19	LU
Flora Lucas Shadwell	7s 6d	W. Wackell	1918	Gone
Harriett	5s	R. Smith	1918-19	LU
Intombi	5s	C. L. Prie	1918	Gone
Isabel	5s	Jude Millgate	1913-19	Sold
Jane	5s	George Mills	1918-24	
Lily	5s	Arthur Robus	1918-24	
Mary Jane	5s	James Robus	1918-23	LU
Mayflower	5s	W. A. Best	1918	LU
Naomi	5s	James Hilder	1918-21	LU
Olive	5s	Edward Mills	1918-24	
Our Boys	5s	Wm. Cutting	1918-23	
Pearl	5s	Wm. Smith	1918/20/23	
Perseverance	7s 6d	Mesher	1918-22	
Renown	10s	Edward Mills	1918-24	
Secret	5s	John Caister	1918-23	
Welcome Home	5s	Rd Cutting	1918-24	
Three Brothers	5s	M. Edwards	1918-24	
Shamrock	5s	R. Smith	1918-19	LU
No name	5s	W. Martin	1919	LU
Conger Eel	5s	J. Chandler	Nil	LU
Fame	5s	J. Jewhurst	Nil	LU
Golden City	5s	S. White	Nil	LU

(LU = Laid up.)

RYE HARBOUR DUES

BOULDER, SAILING AND MOTOR- FISHING BOATS: 1935-

Name		Rate per ¼ yr.		Date	Info.
Uncle Dick	DS	J. Moon	1s	1935-9	Broken up
Zephyr	DS	Page and Smith	1s	1935	Broken up
Small	MB	Old Turks, Iden	5s	1935	Not used
Christine	MB	D. Jarrett	10s	1935-6	Sold
Popsy	SB	G. Blattman	10s	1935-9	
Pipola	SB	P. Lindsay	5s	1935-9	
Small boat		do.	5s	1935	Not used
Mac, now Meteor 11					
	SB	E. Goddard	5s	1935-8	
Whynot	SB	W. Scrivener	5s	1935-9	
Florence	SB	G. Paine	10s	1935-7	Taken away
Janetta	SB	Mrs Manton Graham			
			5s	1935-9	
Curlew	SB	F. Rootes	10s	1935-7	Sold
Tern	SB	Mrs Granville	5s	1935	Not used
Boulder Boat		G. Robus	5s	1935	Not used
Boy Jim	MFB	J. Robus	10s	1935-7	Laid up
Donian	SE	W. R. Weatherseed			
			10s	1935-7	Taken away
Smuggler	SB	R. Burra	10s	1935-7	Lost at sea
First Event	NFB	G. Southerden	10s	1935-8	Sold.
Spinaway	MFB	Mr Meikle	10s	1935-7	Sold.
Owl	SB	C. A. Nichols	10s	1935-9	
Avona	DS	J. Moon	1s	1935-9	
Margaret	MFB	B. Caister	10s	1935	Laid up
Comrade	BB	W. Smith	5s	1935	Laid up
Boulder Boat		E. Pope	5s	1935	Laid up
Happy Return					
	MFB	E. Mills	10s	1935-9	
Janira	MFB	B. Downey	10s	1935-9	
Pearl	MFB	W. Smith	10s	1935	Laid up

Name	Type	Owner	Price	Year	Notes
Mountsfield					
	BB	W. Smith	5s	1935-9 J	
Fame	MFB	S. Sewhurst	10s	1935-6	Laid up
Pride of Rye					
	MB	W. Fletcher	10s	1935-9	
Jubilee Belle					
	SB	Mr Cherry	10s	1935-9	
Olive	BB	A. Mills	5s.	1935-9	
Perkie	BB	A. Mills	5s	1835-9	
Rose	BB	R. Cutting	5s	1935-7	Not used
Waterlily	RB	R. Cutting	5s	1935-5	Now used as pilot's boat
Pampero	Speed boat		10s	1935-6	Laid up
Victory	Lighter	Vidler&Son	£1 1s	1935	Broken up
Mullett	do.	do.	£1 1s	1935	Sold to Mackley & Co
Wear	do.	do.	£1 1s	1935	Sold to Catchment Board
Grit Boat		F. Blackhall	5s	1935-39	
Margaret	BB	E. Mills	5s	1935	Not used
Sprite 11	SB		10s	1935	Laid up
Iron	NFB	G. Southerden	10s	1935-37	
Mandie	SB	E. Bourne	5s	1935-39	
Rowing Boat		Mr Cotton	10s	1935	Not used
Meteor	Smack	H. Crampton	12s 6d	1935-36	
Kent Colebrooke		R. T. Page	12s 6d	1935	Broken up
Three Brothers		C. Fowle	9s 6d	1935-6	
Houseboat		W. R. Weatherseed			
			10s	1835-6	
Torquade	Yacht	E. W. Sawson	£2	1935-6	
White Cloud					
	SB	Mr Velch	10s	1935-8	Not used
Silver Spray					
	SB	Mr Fryer	5s	1935-9	
Marksman	MB		10s	1935-9	
Hit the Deck					
	MB		10s	1935	Taken away
Wendy	SB	Mr Pettit	5s	1935-7	do.
St. Vincent		Mr B. Wilson	5s	1935	Taken away
Rowing Boat		Mr W. Caister	5s	1935	Not used
Mayflower		Mr F. Taylor	10s	1935-6	Laid up

RYE HARBOUR DUES
from DEACON'S ALMANAC 1935

1. On vessels laden with Cargo (except Timber
   or Liquid Oil), entering or departing,
   per Registered ton 6d
2. On Steam or Motor Vessels laden with Timber
   or Liquid Oil, entering or departing,
   per Registered ton 1s 0d
3. On Sailing Ships laden with Timber
   entering, per Registered ton 8d
4. For Sailing Fishing Boats belonging to the
   Port, per Registered Ton per year, payable
   quarterly by agreement.
5. Steam Trawlers or Steam Fishing Vessels
   coming into Harbour, 2/6 per mooring post,
   or, by agreement £2 10s per annum.
6 All Boats under 5 tons, 10/- a year, payable half yearly.
7 Fishing Boats not belonging to the Port
   coming into the Harbour as follows:
   > For each mooring post 2s 6d
   > For Windbound Vessels, for each mooring post 2s 6d

—

DAY TIDE SIGNALS

On the East side of the Harbour are now shown from a mast and
yard in the following manner :-
7ft. water, red flag on yard; 8ft., 1 ball on yard; 9ft., 1 ball on each arm
of yard; 10ft., 1 ball on masthead only; 11ft., 1 ball on masthead, 1 ball
on yard; 12ft., 1 ball on masthead, 1 ball on each arm of yard.

—

NIGHT SIGNALS

7ft., 1 green light; 8ft., 1 red light; 9 ft., 1 red and 1 white light; 10ft.,
white light . . . .

I think you all must agree that this is a most unusual present and thanks of all at the Lifeboat station are extended to James Tysoe.
RICHARD TOLLETT

Look! in the tossing, raging swell
That bubbles like a cauldron straight from hell,
Where men can see their beckoning doom
In depths of black and endless surging seas -
A courage, stout as English oak
Adorns our life boat men who soak
Their Sussex heritage with spray
And launch their tiny craft, 'Away!',
To rescue fools in jeopardy,
Or luckless sailors, just foolhardy,
With scarce a backward look or thought -
They follow in the steps of those who brought
Their ancient boat back near the shore
And lost their lives, all seventeen,
Claimed by the sea - as though, they'd never been.

A view of duty and a glimpse of honour,
High and noble,
Still shocks, inspires and men enable
To carry on where they, the Seventeen have gone.
For them the brave live on.
Their monument, no, only stonish white
In graveyard's solemn light - but bright
In lives that now, at first maroon
Leave wives, and work, a pint, pontoon -
Whatever occupies when duty calls
Is left, to rush to rescue, where the falls
And plumes of sea make bold men weep.
Salute, respect and honour these,
Our life boat men who careful watches keep.

James Tysoe
Rose Cottage,
Rye Harbour.

LOCAL HISTORY GROUPS

1986-1987
Michelle Robus
Kay Beeching
Stephen Tollett
Dean Blanshard
Tracy Champion
Denise Cotterell
John Green
James Kemp
Marie Pawson
Sharon Vidler

1987-1988
Michelle Robus
Kay Beeching
Stephen Tollett
Keith Williams
Samantha Jones
Zena Piggott
Louise Gilchrist
Mark Newnham
James Rosewell
Joseph Taylor
Elizabeth Cox
Joanna Pettifer
Emma Ashbee

1988-1989
Mark Newnham
Nigel Hammond
Gregory Coleman
Loraine Charman
Robert Ramsay
Barnaby Willard
Lisa Carder
Martin Phillips
Lisa Wilson
Lorraine Jury

1989-1990
Nigel Hammond
Gregory Coleman
Jonathon Breeds
James Eldridge
Christopher Apps
Tina Kennard
David Watts
Loraine Charman
Robert Ramsay
Sophie Crofts
Jane Cuthbert
David Standen
Andrew Gainsbury
Christopher Parsons

1990-1991
Loraine Charman
Robert Ramsay
Gregory Coleman
Jonathon Breeds
Andrew Gainsbury

1991-1992
Andrew Gainsbury
Penny Bell
Sarah Booth
Helen Robus
Donna Ripley
Matthew Collison
Steven Carter
Talya Bagwell
Helena Swaine
Phillip Pearce

1992-1993
Sarah Booth
Daryl Balcombe
Steven Field
Rae Newnham
Mark Smyth
Chris Wheeler
Jo Weekes

1993-1994
Vicky Beach
Jason Beckingham
Shelley Case
Julie Ennis
David Giles
Lisa Graham
Marie Hodgson
Jackie Lewis
Ian Potter
Hayley Rozier
Michelle Webb

Heidi Booth
Gina Bridgland
Lee Champion
Kevin Fuller
Lisa Goodsell
Claire Highams
Catherine Jung
Rebecca Mastin
Robin Pschenychka
Chris O'Shaugnessy
Loraine Charman

1994-1995
Vicky Beach
Kevin Fuller
Jackie Lewis
Georgina Pinwill
Lindsay Shipp
Andrew Tomkins

1995-1996
Hannah Brown
Claire Higham
Rosie Head
Samuel Jones
Alison Rowland

Paul Byrne
Laura Farley
Samantha Jones
Jackie Lewis
Steven Beach

Mrs Jo Kirkham, teacher of Geography and History, and Mayor of Rye 1979-1982, is the Co-Ordinator and Editor of the 'Rye Memories Series'